1966

BOOKS BY

RICHARD H. S. CROSSMAN

A Nation Reborn

Richard H. S. Crossman

A NATION
REBORN

A Personal Report on the Roles Played by
Weizmann, Bevin and Ben-Gurion
in the Story of Israel

NEW YORK ATHENEUM PUBLISHERS

1960

To the living

B.-G.

in memory of the dead

C. W.

Foreword

LAST APRIL I spent a fortnight at Rehovoth in Israel, finding out from the nuclear physicists, the biochemists, the mathematicians and the other research Fellows of the Weizmann Institute what it feels like to live the life of a pure scientist in a tiny, isolated Western democracy, cut off from its Arab neighbours by a frontier of hatred. Sometimes, of an evening, I would stand on the roof of the Casa San Martin, the VIP hostel where my wife and I were entertained in such tranquil comfort, and look across the heavy green orange groves to the pale Judaean hills and the Jordan frontier a few miles away. Cross that frontier, I used to say to myself, and one would have to travel three quarters of the way round the world—as far as California—before one found another academic institution where Western science and Western scientific humanism flourish quite naturally as part of a free nation's life.

The Weizmann Institute is not merely pre-eminent for the quality of its scientific output. It is also a living community, whose buildings and gardens have been planned and tended with such exquisite care that the Israeli, who are even untidier than the British, have learnt to put their cigarette ends in their pockets instead of throwing them on the flower beds. I felt wonderfully at home inside this tiny international enclosure, which breathed the spirit of Plato's original Academy. When I hadn't an appointment with one of the scientists, I would spend the morning in the beautiful buildings where the Weizmann Archives are housed and tempt the chief archivist, Mr. Boris Guriel, to reveal to me some more of his secrets. For I was preparing myself to deliver the fourth Chaim Weizmann Memorial Lectures in the Humanities, and it is the text of these lectures that forms the basis of this book. All the unpublished documents I have quoted, either in full or in excerpt, I found in the Weizmann Archives and I have used them by kind permission of Mrs. Chaim Weizmann, widow of the first President of Israel, and of Mr. Meyer Weisgal, Chairman of the Editorial Board. I hope they at least give a foretaste of the historical riches which will be revealed when the official life and correspondence of Chaim Weizmann are finally published.*

The lectures (sponsored by the Yad Chaim Weizmann) were given on three successive evenings, under the chairmanship respectively of Mr. Meyer Weisgal, Chairman of Yad Chaim Weizmann; Mr. David Horowitz, Governor of the Bank of Israel; and Mr. Moshe Shamir, the Hebrew author and

---

* The documents of which I have given only extracts in the text are printed in full in the Appendix at the end of the book, either in the original English or in a translation which Mr. Boris Guriel has personally authorised.

playwright. I delivered them in the impressive Michael and Anna Wix Auditorium, which stands across the road from the Weizmann Archives and faces the sunken gardens dedicated to the memory of Sigmund Gestetner. In Israel, unlike Britain, a lecture is an occasion and, though Rehovoth is more than ten miles from Tel Aviv and forty from Jerusalem, the audience was terrifyingly numerous and distinguished.

In introducing me on the first evening, Mr. Weisgal described me as a "brilliant intellectual," though he knows full well that this compliment is the kiss of death for a Labour politician in Britain today! But his object, I fancy, was not to blight an already blighted political career but to dissipate the impression that Anglo-Saxon anti-intellectualism has spread to Israel. One of the signs that the Israeli nation is now achieving manhood is the entry into key positions in all walks of life of a home-born generation of sabras*—sometimes accused by their elders of having rid themselves not only of the complexes but of the intellectualism of the Jewish Diaspora. If his object in inviting me to deliver these lectures was to demonstrate the falseness of this charge, he must have been gratified by his success. For how much further could a learned institution go in toleration of the nonconformist, the rebel and the awkward cuss than to invite the man who "stabbed Bevin in the back" to say freely and without inhibition what he

* "Sabra," literally cactus, is the word used to describe any Jew born and bred in Israel.

felt about the most controversial problems of Zionism and Anglo-Jewish relations? Moreover, the
lengthy questioning and discussion which followed
each lecture dissipated any idea that the new generation of politicians and writers lacks the dialectical
passion and argumentative skill of its Zionist fathers.
When we were finally pushed out of the Auditorium, a bunch of us would continue the argument,
stumbling in a crowd through the fragrant night to
some hospitable nearby house, where no time limit
was imposed and no holds barred. When I came to
study the text of the lectures I had delivered, I
realised that they were thin indeed when contrasted
with the content of those fierce disputations that followed them. In this book the lectures have been
completely recast and I have sought to work into the
text something of what I learnt from the hours of
passionate conversation which made my stay at Rehovoth a spiritual oasis in the arid and bumpy desert
of political life.

Contents

I

The Zionist Vision

CHAIM WEIZMANN

By what right do I, an English Gentile, claim to talk about Weizmann's Zionist faith? My answer is that in the course of this century the histories of Great Britain and of the Jewish people have been tragically yet providentially intertwined—and the man chiefly responsible for this was Chaim Weizmann. As for myself, I can claim expert knowledge neither of Zionism nor of the Middle East. My mind was empty, if not open, when I was pitched into the Palestine problem by Ernest Bevin's decision to appoint me, in the autumn of 1945, one of the two British M.P.'s on the Anglo-American Commission of Enquiry. Since Mr. Bevin was a careful man and was hopeful that this Commission's report would help his own plans for Palestine, it is not difficult to conclude that I started our hundred-and-twenty-day investigation without any bias in favour of Zionism!

Looking back now, I can see that Mr. Bevin was playing for time; the main function of our Commission was to postpone for a hundred and twenty days the very awkward decision that faced him. It was irritating to discover that I had taken part in a mere time-wasting operation, but I can be grateful to Ernest Bevin for two things. By sending me to Palestine, he made me first an observer and then a partici-

3

pant in the birth of a new nation, the most thrilling and probably the most useful episode in my political life. Secondly, it was he who unwittingly forged my only intimate friendship with a great statesman. It was thanks to Ernest Bevin that I came to know Chaim Weizmann during the last, most tragic and yet grandest episode of his career.

I

When I consider the birth of Israel, therefore, my natural starting point is the personality of Weizmann. I do not think of him as the first President of Israel—or, indeed, as an Israeli at all—but as the leader of international Jewry, the one great statesman thrown up by the Zionist movement since Herzl founded it. Unlike Moses, Weizmann died after he reached the Promised Land, and his body lies at Rehovoth. Yet spiritually he remained on Pisgah, the last of those who prophesied an Israel yet unborn.

In considering Weizmann's Zionism, it is natural for an Englishman to start with the letter he wrote as a boy of eleven to his schoolmaster in Pinsk. Before I visited the Weizmann Archives, I had read a translation of this letter in which the text had been watered down at one vital point in order to soothe American susceptibilities. The more I study it, the more this letter fascinates me, and I spent a whole morning with the chief archivist, Mr. Boris Guriel, before we were able to agree that the following text, if inelegant, is reasonably accurate.

My teacher, my mentor, Schlomo Sokolovsky, I am sending you one of my ideas so that you can see about the Society of Lovers of Zion and Jerusalem in our land. How great and lofty was the idea which inspired our brother Jews to found this Society! Through it we can save our downtrodden and despondent brethren who are scattered in all corners of the world and have no place in which to pitch their tents. We are being persecuted everywhere and the Jew is a burden on all people, and on all the kings of Europe generally and on the king of Russia in particular. Yet this may be the beginning of our redemption. We must therefore support this esteemed Society and we must thank all the supporters of this Society, such as Dr. Yassinovsky and Dr. Pinsker and all who rallied underneath the flag of this Society. But we must also thank two Jewish patriots, and they are Moses Montefiore and Rothschild. Finally, we must thank this Society, because we are able to see what lies before us and the evil which threatens us. Therefore the obligation lies upon us to find some place of refuge. Because even in America, where knowledge prevails, they will persecute us, and in all the countries of Africa and especially in the State of Morocco they will persecute us and have no mercy upon us. So let us carry our banner to Zion. Let us return to our original mother, on whose knees we were reared. For why should we expect mercy from the kings of Europe, that they should, in their pity for us, give us a resting place? In vain. All have decided that the Jew is doomed to death, but England will have mercy on us. Nonetheless, let us turn to Zion. Jews, to Zion let us go.

From me, your pupil, CHAIM WEIZMANN.

How did a boy of eleven, living in a remote village of the Pale, foresee all that? It is tempting for an Englishman to accept the letter as it stands, without seeking a rational explanation. Yet what looks like a miraculous prophecy is at least partially elucidated by a passage in Weizmann's autobiography. In his first chapter, Weizmann describes his childhood at Motol, where his father was a *transportierer,* who cut and hauled the timber and got it floated down the Vistula to Danzig. Next door lived Grandfather, and when Weizmann was five he went to live with him and listened, rapt, to the old man's stories.

I was particularly impressed by the visit of Sir Moses Montefiore to Russia—one of his innumerable journeys on behalf of his people. That particular visit had taken place only a generation or so before my birth, but the story was already a legend. Indeed Sir Moses Montefiore was himself, though then still living, already a legend. He was to live on until 1885, to the fabulous age of one hundred and one years. On the occasion of which my grandfather used to tell me, Sir Moses came to Vilna, one of the oldest and most

6

illustrious Jewish settlements in Russia, and the Jews . . . came out to welcome him . . . unharnessed the horses and dragged the carriage of Sir Moses Montefiore in solemn procession through the streets.*

This passage seems to me to explain, but not to explain away, the prophecy contained in the letter. Already by the age of eleven, Weizmann's thinking and emotions had taken on the Zionist pattern which, when fully developed, enabled him to negotiate the Balfour Declaration. What we see here, in fact, is not so much a prophecy as a childish anticipation of the grown man's philosophy of life. Weizmann's Zionism was not rooted in Western, far less in British, ideas but in the life of the Russian Jews under Tsarist tyranny. Because as a boy he was at best a second-class citizen in the Russian state and at worst a victim of persecution, he grew up completely free from that double loyalty which so many of his Western Jewish contemporaries felt. A Jew forbidden to live outside the Pale and treated by the state as a foreign body could feel no Russian patriotism. His only patriotism was a purely Jewish patriotism, and the only country which he could call his own was the land to which, as he read every day in his Bible, the Jews were bound to return.

For a Jew growing up in Britain or America, Zion-

* Chaim Weizmann, *Trial and Error* (New York, Harper & Brothers, 1949), p. 7. Reprinted by permission of Harper & Brothers.

7

ism is today a philanthropic cause. For the boy Weizmann, at the end of the last century, it was the only hope. Already, writing to his schoolmaster, he could talk quite naturally about Palestine as his National Home. Already, seeing the weakness of his own people, he could conclude that the return to Zion would not take place without the assistance of a great power. But with all the world, including the new power of America, apparently against them, what power would rescue the Jews? How natural that this little boy should think of the remote country from which Sir Moses Montefiore had come to relieve their distress! This is not the view of Great Britain which a boy brought up in an assimilated Western family would have obtained. No! The idea of an island of freedom and chivalry, far away in the Atlantic, is precisely the kind of romantic notion which lightened the darkness of the Jewish Pale.

II

Seven years later Weizmann made his first journey abroad. At the age of nineteen he found himself at the terrible school of Dr. Barness of Pfungstadt. He had already acquired the inner core of his Zionist outlook: all his political and spiritual aspirations were centred on a physical and actual return of the Jewish people to Zion and the creation of a Jewish national state in Palestine. In Germany, however, a new and important element was added. Weizmann arrived at Pfungstadt with a passion for Western science and a worship of Western freedom. Now his devotion to Western civilisation was to be counter-balanced by a hatred for the assimilated Jew and, in particular, for the wealthy, super-patriotic German Jew.

Pfungstadt was my introduction to one of the queerest chapters in Jewish history: that of the assimilated Jews of Germany, then in the high summer of their illusory security, and mightily proud of it. . . . Dr. Barness was completely as-similated, and described himself as "a German of the Mosaic persuasion." He took his Judaism to mean that in all respects save that of a religious ritual he was as German, in culture, background and personality, as any descendant of the Cerusci. . . . Even Dr. Barness could not ignore the evi-dence of Jew-hatred about him. But he regarded it as the result of a slight misunderstanding. If some Germans were anti-Semitically inclined, it was be-cause they did not know the sterling qualities of the Jews, as exemplified in Dr. Barness and his like. They had to be told—that was all. A little enlightenment, judiciously applied, and anti-Semi-tism would simply vanish.

With all my youthful naïveté I just could not stomach Dr. Barness' rather fatuous and self-satis-fied philosophy of anti-Semitism; and though it was shared by all the teachers in the school, I did not yet suspect that it was a characteristic of most of German Jewry. . . . At the time I only knew—when I began, with an increasing grasp of the language, to understand what he was talking about —that he caused me the acutest discomfort. Without a philosophy of history or of anti-Semitism, I felt clearly enough that Dr. Barness was an intellectual coward and a toady. . . . I remember how, shortly after my arrival, one of the teachers asked me what nationality I was; and when I answered, *"Ein Russischer Jude"* (a Russian Jew), he stared at me, then went off into gales of laughter. He had never heard of such a thing. A German, yes. A Russian, yes. Judaism, yes. But a Russian Jew! That was to him the height of the ridiculous.*

There was nothing contradictory or inconsistent in combining a love of Western ideas with a contempt for Western assimilation. Anyone from Motol was bound to regard as a traitor the Frankfurter or Berliner who denied his Jewishness and sought to pretend that he was a German. What distinguished Weizmann from most of the other Russian Zionists was his recognition that to create a Jewish nation in Palestine would involve something more than transplanting the Jew from the Pale and plunking him down in Palestine, with all his narrow orthodoxy and blinkered outlook. The new Jewish nation, in Weizmann's view, would combine all the vibrant Jewishness of family life in the Pale with the best of the scientific and democratic culture of the West.

* *Trial and Error*, pp. 31-32.

The aim of the true Zionist, therefore, must be not to assimilate himself to the Western democracies but to translate into Jewish national terms their science and their freedom.

The fact that Weizmann combined a love of Western civilisation with a hatred of assimilation explains one puzzling aspect of his character, which struck me on my first meeting with him in Rehovoth. I was confronted with a personality who combined the fanaticism and power of Lenin with the sophisticated charm of Disraeli. Even more puzzling, here was a Jew who obviously preferred the company of British Gentiles to that of assimilated Jews. As I got to know him, it became even clearer that we English were regarded as Goyim, for whom allowances must be made, whereas he never forgave the shortcomings of the Jew—especially the German Jew—who should have known better. For to Weizmann every Jew was a potential Zionist, and those whose Jewish patriotism was qualified by any other national loyalty were to be pitied or despised. Certainly he was prepared to collect their money for the cause, but they could never earn his complete respect. Since very few Western Jews passed this test, it was natural enough that Weizmann should feel more at home with honest-to-God Englishmen, Americans and Frenchmen.

III

The structure of Weizmann's world outlook was completed at Geneva, where he taught chemistry and had his first clash with the kind of "progressive" thinkers who believe that the problem of anti-Semitism can be disposed of by the bland assertion, "All men are brothers." This outlook was prevalent among the Russian students in Switzerland, most of whom were ardent members of the Social Democratic Party, then dominated by Lenin. One of the basic principles of Russian Social Democracy and later of Russian Communism was that there was no real difference between a black man and a white man or between a Jew and a Gentile. Such differences were part of the superstructure of bourgeois nationalism and would disappear after the revolution. In Germany, Weizmann had acquired a radical contempt for the rich Jews who sought to assimilate themselves into the Western Christian community. In Geneva, he acquired an equally radical contempt for the Jewish intellectuals who denied their real Jewishness for the sake of an abstract theory of world revolution.

One of the stories which I made him repeat to me until I almost knew it by heart was the occasion at Bern when he challenged the Socialists who dominated the Russian student organisation to a debate on Zionism. In order to make sure of victory, these students had invited some of the most prominent

Russian Social Democrats in exile to speak. So fierce was the struggle that it was protracted for three days and two nights on end, until the Marxists could bring up their reinforcements from Berlin. In speech after speech they proved conclusively that Zionism was a vulgar bourgeois heresy, incompatible with the principles of dialectical materialism, the doctrine of the class war and the aim of the classless society.

Owing to the *numerus clausus* imposed in Russian universities, a very large number of the students present were Jews, compelled to come West in order to graduate. For them the topic of debate was not abstract theory but an *Existenzfrage*. Most of them were miserably poor, condemned to a life of second-class citizenship in a benighted and backward Tsarist Empire. All of them dreamed of a revolution which would usher in a new world. But what kind of revolution? Should they put aside all differences of colour, race and nationality and join the oppressed proletariat in a world revolution? That was the tremendous future presented to them by Lenin and Plekhanov and Axelrod. Or should they follow this tall, unknown lecturer in chemistry, who coolly informed them that the world revolution was escapist nonsense; that the only way a Jew could achieve his own or his people's freedom was by the return to Zion and the transformation of Palestine into a Jewish national state?

When the debate ended, no vote was taken, but on the next day Weizmann was able to found the first student Zionist organisation in Switzerland.

13

Among those he had converted was a handsome girl from Rostov-on-Don, who was studying medicine and whom he helped by translating lectures into Russian. Vera, who later became his wife, had been brought up outside the Pale as a Russian rather than a Jew. Whereas Chaim was born into Zionism, she was a Zionist by intellectual conversion, a brand saved from the fire of assimilation by her fiancé.

The years at Geneva were the period when Weizmann's philosophy (as distinct from his policies and programme) reached its full development. Nothing essential was added to it either when he settled in Britain or by his visits to Palestine. From now on he was a "concrete" revolutionary, set apart from the other Zionist politicians by his conscious dislike of what he contemptuously dismissed as "abstract internationalism"—under which he condemned not only Eastern Marxism but Western liberalism as well. Both outlooks he regarded as vitiated by a refusal to face the basic fact on which Zionism is founded—the essential unassimilable Jewishness of the Jew, and the hostility which this must arouse so long as the Jew lives in a foreign community.

Anti-Semitism, he used to say to me, is a bacillus which every Gentile carries with him wherever he goes and however often he denies it. Like other bacilli, it may remain quiescent and harmless for years. But once the right conditions are created, the bacilli multiply and the epidemic breaks out. The condition for an outbreak of overt anti-Semitism in any nation is that the number of Jews should rise beyond the safety level of that particular nation. Hence the only radical cure for anti-Semitism is the creation of the Jewish state. At our first meeting, which lasted most of the way through the night, Weizmann outlined this theory to me and asked me whether I was anti-Semitic. When I said, "Of course," I felt that our friendship had begun. For if a Gentile denied his latent anti-Semitism, Weizmann concluded that he must either be lying or, even worse, deceiving himself. In his view the only honest attitude for a Gentile to adopt was to admit his unconscious prejudice against Jews, consciously make allowances for it and so ensure that it did not influence his behaviour.

I V

Browsing in the Rehovoth Archives, I was more and more impressed by the radicalism of Weizmann's outlook. Gradually, since he had died and my memory of him had begun to fade, I had begun to absorb the view, preached by so many important people, that Weizmann was a bourgeois politician who stood well Right of Centre. There is some truth in this view, as I shall show later, if we consider only his attitude to the British Empire. But this was not a central part of his philosophy, which remained rooted in the life of the Jewish masses, exiled from their homeland and deprived of their nationhood. Here Weizmann was a radical, since he saw clearly that the creation of a Jewish nation in Palestine would require a social revolution that would completely transform the urban, commercial way of life forced on the Jews of the Diaspora. He was always prepared to accept any social policies, however extreme, if they could be shown to assist the settlement of Jews in Palestine.

Another factor which strengthened the radicalism of his outlook was his rationalism and devotion to scientific method. Among a people which had preserved its Jewishness only by strict observance of religious traditions and religious ceremony, his rationalist contempt for every kind of superstition always struck me as very remarkable. At first I felt there was a contradiction between his delight in dancing the hora and the delight he also took in baiting the rabbis about kosher food. But later I came to realise the validity of his distinction between an ancient hygiene, now recognised as unscientific, and a dance which, though it apparently derives from Eastern Europe, perfectly expresses the Jewish national character. Scientific Zionism, in his view, requires that the former, which is nothing but a taboo, should be stripped by derision of the awe with which it is surrounded, whereas the other must be lovingly preserved.

Some writers have tried to separate Weizmann's science from his Zionism and to treat him as a man with two separate careers and life interests. Actually his devotion to science and to Zionism was a single passion, already fused during his period at Geneva into a single philosophy, which may be described either as scientific or as organic Zionism. I can best illustrate its main characteristic by describing the impression he made on me on the first occasion when I met him face to face. It was in Jerusalem in 1946, when he gave his testimony before the Anglo-American Commission. One of the most controversial issues which our terms of reference required us to investigate was President Truman's suggestion that a hundred thousand survivors of the gas chambers should immediately be granted certificates of entry into Palestine. One of my American colleagues —Frank Buxton—put the question to him. "Now, Dr. Weizmann, could you get the hundred thousand in within twelve months?" I remember very distinctly what happened. Weizmann paused and thought. Then he said, "I'm not sure about twelve months, but certainly we could within one or two years." I can still see the fury and perturbation on the faces of the Zionist delegation sitting behind Weizmann. Here was their leader showing doubt and hesitation when he should have answered straightaway, "Of course. At once. In twelve months we can do it."

Yet when the Commission met that evening in private, we discovered that the one fact that stuck out of all that day's testimony was this remark of Weizmann's. So far from weakening the Jewish position, it had impressed us all, because Weizmann was the first witness to show some scientific, objective doubt. Everyone else, Arab and Jew, had been cocksure and glib, and if they were uncertain of

17

anything, felt a duty to suppress it. Only Weizmann was prepared to say, simply and openly, "I'm not quite sure." And this example of Weizmann's objectivity made us take the rest of his evidence, and that of the other Jews, far more seriously.

Listening to Weizmann that day made me think of Tomáš Masaryk—another democratic revolutionary of the same generation and of the same calibre. He too combined what Weizmann used to describe as a "blinkered nationalism" with a scientific passion for truth. Indeed, he wrote a whole book in order to prove that the most popular nationalist Czechoslovak legend was based on a forgery. When some of his colleagues complained that he was destroying their propaganda, he replied, "Truth is the only propaganda I believe in." The authority of Chaim Weizmann as the leader of Jewry in exile was of the same kind as that of Tomáš Masaryk in his struggle to liberate the Czechoslovak people. Both men were democratic revolutionaries, in the strict sense of both words. They had a simple faith that freedom, truth, equality and liberty are ideals which can only be realised when a people is free to rule itself freely, and they believed this without the complications and reservations of our times. For in their view the truth and the good of the community were not merely compatible but essential to each other. It was this which made them both such balanced, serene personalities and enabled them to exert great authority over the movements they led without becoming autocrats or dictators.

V

So we come to the period which naturally interests me most—Weizmann's long sojourn in Britain. Whoever undertakes the official biography will have to hack his way through a jungle of legend before he writes these chapters. Working in unnatural alliance, many of Weizmann's British admirers and some of his bitterest Jewish enemies have combined to assert that by living in Britain he became an Anglicised member of Anglo-Jewry, agonisingly divided between his prime loyalty to Jewry and his secondary loyalty to the country whose passport he was so proud to bear. I saw a good deal of Weizmann at a time when Anglo-Jewish relations were at their worst, and it is my considered conclusion that this account of his relationship to Britain is based on a complete misunderstanding. It is true that when he actually set foot in the country of which he had written so romantically at the age of eleven, Weizmann was not disappointed. If a Jew had to live as a foreigner among a strange people, then England was the best country of exile in the world. It is also true that he formed almost as strong a dislike for the wealthy, assimilated English Jews as he had for the German Jews, and treated them with a sardonic contempt which he never displayed toward the English Gentile. What is not true is that he ever became sufficiently Anglicised to feel that "double loyalty" which so worried his anti-Zionist opponents among British Jewry.

Here again, as we saw in studying his schoolboy letter, the first beginnings foreshadowed clearly the shape of things to come. Before he finally settled in Manchester, Weizmann made a very brief visit to London. It occurred in 1904, the year after the Sixth Congress, in which Theodor Herzl had read the famous letter from the British government, signed by Lord Lansdowne, offering the Jews, as an alternative to Palestine, an autonomous territory in what was then Uganda and is now Kenya. No final decision was taken, but the Congress was terribly divided and Weizmann was among those who challenged the leadership as a *Neinsager*. It was in this capacity that he was sent to investigate the Uganda proposal.

There were two episodes in this brief visit characteristic of his whole future relationship with Britain. The first took place in the Foreign Office. Weizmann had been given a letter of introduction to Lord Percy (brother of Lord Eustace Percy), who was then in charge of African affairs.

Lord Percy was the first English statesman I met. He was a man in the thirties, with the finely chiseled features of his family, courteous and affable in manner, and obviously well informed. He asked me a great deal about the Zionist movement, and expressed boundless astonishment that the Jews should ever so much as have considered the

Uganda proposal, which he regarded as imprac-
tical on the one hand, and, on the other, a denial
of the Jewish religion. Himself deeply religious,
he was bewildered by the thought that Jews could
even entertain the idea of any other country than
Palestine as the center of their revival; and he was
delighted to hear from me that there were so many
Jews who had categorically refused. He said: "If
I were a Jew I would not give a halfpenny for this
proposition!" *

Weizmann's previous experience had been limited to
Russian, German and Swiss officialdom. He was surprised and captivated by Lord Percy's informality
and candour. That an official representative of a
great power, formally pledged to the Uganda policy,
should advise him to turn it down seemed to him to
prove that the spirit of old Sir Moses Montefiore was
as strong as ever. This episode roused in him that
fondness for the British ruling class which, in the
case of Lord Balfour, was to develop into an exqui-
sitely balanced personal friendship.

The second episode was a meeting with a very
different kind of Englishman, Sir William Evans
Gordon, M.P. This is how Weizmann described it.

Sir William Evans Gordon—the father of the
Aliens Bill . . . was generally regarded as respon-
sible for all the difficulties placed in the way of
Jewish immigrants into England. . . . The Aliens

* *Trial and Error*, p. 89.

Bill in England, and the movement which grew up around it were natural phenomena which might have been foreseen. They were a repetition of a phenomenon only too familiar in our history. Whenever the quantity of Jews in any country reaches the saturation point, that country reacts against them. . . . The reaction . . . cannot be looked upon as anti-Semitism in the ordinary or vulgar sense of that word; it is a universal social and economic concomitant of Jewish immigration, and we cannot shake it off.

Sir William Evans Gordon had no particular anti-Jewish prejudices. . . . I am fairly sure he would equally have opposed the mass influx of any foreign element; but . . . no other foreign element pressed for admission in such numbers. . . . Evans Gordon gave me some insight into the psychology of the settled citizen, and though my views of immigration naturally were in sharp conflict with his, we discussed these problems in a quite objective . . . way.*

Such tolerance of a British "blimp" is all the more breathtaking when we read, a few paragraphs later, the following assessment of British Jewry.

Zionism in England reflected the general critical condition of the movement at its worst. . . . Zionism at this time was acquiring a peculiar savor; it tended to be transformed into a rather low-grade

* *Trial and Error*, pp. 90-91.

British patriotism—a British patriotism based on an imaginary attachment to an imaginary country which nobody had seen and nobody knew.*

When the young Weizmann talked to Lord Percy and Sir William Evans Gordon, he knew not a word of English and was completely ignorant of the British way of life. Yet we can already observe, in his methods of handling these English gentlemen, the two qualities which were later to serve him so well in negotiating the Balfour Declaration. He always had the knack of being courteous without seeming obsequious and he was able to do this without play-acting, precisely because he always felt himself to be representing Jewry to a strange people whose help he needed and whose foibles he studied with a detached fascination.

VI

In 1904 Dr. Weizmann and his fiancée, after many doubts and hesitations, decided to settle in Britain. He arrived, as we have seen, with a deep suspicion of British Jewry and an almost dangerously open mind towards the rest of the British people. This open-mindedness made him an instantaneous success when he arrived in Manchester with an appointment as a lecturer in chemistry but still with no knowledge of English. And that success deepened when his wife, having qualified for the

* Ibid., p. 94.

second time, and in yet another language, as a doctor, became a British medical officer of health.

The mistake of most historians is hindsight—the interpretation of events in terms of a future unknown by the participants. How tempting it is, for example, to believe that one, at least, of Weizmann's motives in coming to England was an uncanny premonition that the British government would one day hold the key to Palestine and that London, therefore, was where Zionism should make its headquarters! There is no evidence to support this view. The truth is that Weizmann went to Britain because Britain seemed to provide the best chance for him as an ambitious young chemist. Once he had settled in Manchester, he concentrated on his academic career, and the famous talk with Balfour, which occurred during the 1906 general election, was an isolated incident. Balfour found it fascinating, but I very much doubt whether Weizmann, at the time, thought it would lead to anything important. So far from anticipating the conditions which would lead to the Balfour Declaration, we find him, on several occasions before 1914, considering the possibility of moving to Palestine—or even back to Germany. For though in retrospect he came to regard his time at Manchester University as a happy comradeship with Rutherford and Alexander, the realities were rather different. Despite his outstanding ability as a chemist, he was passed over by his professor, who, in 1913, for reasons obviously tinged with anti-Semitism, refused to support his undoubted claim to a professorship. Weizmann was so downcast by this gross injustice that he seriously thought of going to Berlin, a decision from which he was only deflected by his wife, who blankly refused to give up her job as a health officer.

Nor is there any contemporary evidence to suggest that in this period he revealed the statesmanship he was later to show. Here, to remind us of the real man, is a recollection of Louis Lipsky, which describes him in 1913 at the Vienna Zionist Congress.

Dr. Weizmann stood in the rear of the hall, where the caucuses were held, his eyes half closed, listening, rarely speaking. He was a shrewd debater, good at repartee, but there was no drive in him at Vienna. He seemed to be listening, to be waiting. There were no intimations of a coming world struggle. The First World War projected Dr. Weizmann into the political field. There was no formal decision. He was drawn into the place which the official leadership should have taken, but was unable, by reason of the war, to take. Dr. Weizmann realised that it was to this fateful moment that he had looked forward from his early days in Switzerland when he read *Daniel Deronda,* and so he became absorbed. The experience transformed him. He passed from the internal world of Zionism to the external world of politics. His public addresses in England now revealed a statesman's approach to the Jewish problem. He was conscious of the world platform on which he stood.

He now began to speak as if the great Jewish past were using him as its medium. He had banished the trivial and held firmly to the eternal.*

It was the First World War that made Weizmann great. For greatness in a statesman is not something intrinsic. To achieve it, a politician must have the good fortune to be presented with an opportunity which exactly matches all his qualities. Some *could* have become great if the opportunity had come their way, and there are even more nonentities who get the opportunity and fail. What made Weizmann great was that everything he had thought and done before World War I fitted him perfectly for the moment which no one, including himself, had anticipated. Viewed in retrospect, the story looks providential and Weizmann's conduct has an appearance of foresight and of calculating shrewdness. What foresight, for example, before the war broke out, to have proved himself a "good security risk" by quarrelling with the German Jews about the Haifa Technion! How shrewd, in 1914, to cut off all correspondence with the Zionists in Berlin, although Berlin was still the headquarters of world Zionism! In fact, of course, these actions were not calculated and showed no foresight. Weizmann's spontaneous display of anti-Germanism quite unwittingly enabled the British security authorities to clear him

* *Chaim Weizmann: Statesman, Scientist, Builder of the Jewish Commonwealth,* Meyer Weisgal, ed. (New York, Dial Press, 1944), p. 167. Reprinted by permission of the publisher.

as a foreign resident who could be trusted to undertake secret work on explosives for the Admiralty,
and so brought him into contact with Lloyd George.
So, too, his hatred of Russian Tsarism, which at the
beginning of the war was something of an embar-
rassment, helped him greatly at the time when the
Balfour Declaration was being discussed. In 1917,
after the Russian Revolution, British politicians were
deeply impressed by the Russian Jew who for three
years had told them they could not rely on the
Tsar.

So we come to the moment when—the period of
waiting over—the opportunity comes and fits the
man as closely as a glove. In 1917, owing to a completely unforeseen concatenation of circumstances,
this second-rank Zionist politician was able to take
over the leadership of world Zionism and make a
pact with the British Empire for a National Home
in Palestine. I am pretty sure that when the appointment with destiny came, Chaim Weizmann had no
doubts or uncertainties. Unlike Churchill, he had
not foreseen, far less planned, his moment of greatness. But when it came, he accepted it with the same
kind of quiet confidence that Sir Winston felt when,
in 1940, he was made Prime Minister and slept
quietly (as he tells us in his war memoirs) for the
first time in years.

VII

What were the motives that prompted the British
government to issue the Balfour Declaration? Weiz-

mann himself has disposed of some of the sillier
"explanations." The silliest perhaps is the theory
that Lloyd George was the prime mover and did it
mainly as a reward for Weizmann's services and in
order to win over the American Jews. As Weizmann
has pointed out, so far from winning them over,
British support for Zionism alienated wealthy American Jewry, as it alienated wealthy British Jewry. It
would be more sensible to suggest that the British
government was wooing the support of the Russian
Jews at this critical period of the Russian Revolution! Another school of historians tells us that the
real motives were strategic: the British government
needed a stronghold north of the Suez Canal from
which to secure communications with India. Again
Weizmann has exploded this fallacy by reminding
us that up to the very last moment the British government was extremely reluctant to take over the
Palestine Mandate. Some farsighted officials certainly
saw the strategic advantages of the Declaration, but
these advantages were not the motive that prompted
it.

I have come to the conclusion that, as so often in
politics, the most obvious explanation is the nearest
to the truth. For slightly different reasons, Balfour,
Lloyd George and Milner all felt under an obligation, in the moment of Allied victory, to do something for oppressed Jewry. It was the achievement
of Weizmann to convince them that the one thing
worth doing and the one thing which, under his
leadership, had now become practicable was the

establishment of the National Home. Other motives —the strategic calculations, the influence on American Jewry, the effect on Russian-Jewish morale— were, I believe, at most secondary factors.

When he was persuading Balfour, Lloyd George and Milner to take this momentous step, how did Weizmann envisage his goal? Strangely enough, there is no answer to be found in the Archives at Rehovoth. Once or twice he had remarked to friends that the Jewish state ought to be rather like Switzerland. But in all his years as an active Zionist, Weizmann had never bothered to consider seriously the constitution, the party system or the kind of democracy a Jewish nation would require.

This refusal to consider hypothetical questions and political problems in the abstract was characteristic of Weizmann's organic Zionism. Although he will be remembered as the creator of the Balfour Declaration, he had a deep scepticism about manifestoes and formal declarations and was constantly chiding his followers for attaching to them an undue importance. Hence we can say that it was owing to Weizmann's deliberate policy that the construction of the Jewish state was undertaken without any blueprint or advance planning. For his belief was in action. He held that once immigration began, the Jewish community in Palestine would begin to evolve spontaneously and organically its own social and political institutions. Those institutions could not be prefabricated by Zionist politicians and planted ready-made in Palestine. They could grow only on the soil of

Israel. So, too, no one could evolve a theory of Jewish democracy outside Palestine and then tell the Yishuv how to conduct its affairs. A genuinely Jewish democracy could only emerge from the struggle of Jews living in their National Home.

Today Weizmann's pragmatism may sound obvious and unoriginal. Yet until the mid-nineteen-thirties it was an attitude which had to be defended against the "Declarationists," who said, "It's no good sending people to Palestine unless you have worked out in advance what they are to do and have published it in a manifesto."

It has been suggested that Weizmann's refusal to theorise was something he had learnt from Britain. There is as little evidence for this view as there is for the suggestion that he learnt anything from British democracy. When I was reading in the Rehovoth Archives, I asked to be shown any references in Weizmann's letters either to British politics or to social conditions in Lancashire, where he lived for so many years. One single letter was found for me, in which he mentions to his wife the terribly sad look of the workers as they go into a factory. But that is all. When I learnt this, I couldn't help contrasting Weizmann's concentration on the plight of his own Jewish people with the attitude of another foreigner who lived for many years in Manchester, Friedrich Engels. Engels came to Lancashire as a cotton manufacturer, but as the collaborator of Karl Marx he concerned himself passionately with the condition of the workers and, as we all know, the Marx-Engels analysis of class war was worked out in terms of Lancashire. Weizmann had just as acute a mind and, when he was dealing with his own people, was just as interested in social conditions and social policies. But, unlike Marx and Engels, he did not feel moved by the condition of the workers in Lancashire, because they were not *his* workers and the problem was not *his* problem. Marx and Engels were self-conscious internationalists who believed in the unity of the working class. He was a self-conscious Jewish nationalist who believed that the Jewish worker of the Diaspora was separated by his Jewishness from the workers around him. That is why he conducted himself throughout his sojourn in Britain as a stranger and always refused to interfere or even to interest himself in British domestic politics, except insofar as they affected the Palestine question. The only obligation he felt was to persuade British politicians of all parties to espouse the Jewish cause.

VIII

This indifference to British social conditions and detachment from British domestic politics goes some way to explain the contradiction between his radical role in Zionist politics and the acquiescent attitude he adopted towards British imperialism. When Weizmann was handling problems of immigration into Palestine, he was not shocked by any proposal, however extreme it might appear, if it could be shown

to assist in settlement on the land. Many Jewish
leaders in the West—in particular, many wealthy
donors—were appalled by the idea of the *kibbutz*
and wrote off collective settlements as "rank Communism." Weizmann, however, backed it enthusiastically because he saw in it a method of turning
Jewish intellectuals into pioneers and thus breaking
the urban, commercial tradition of his people. His
own life was too successful an example of private
enterprise to give him much sympathy for orthodox
state Socialism. But he accepted socialised agriculture, at least as a temporary expedient, because he
rightly recognised that a method must be found for
farming land on which no profit could be shown
for many years. Land nationalisation was another
concept which shocked some Jewish leaders. Once
again, Weizmann accepted it as the best way of
establishing the central land-purchasing authority
essential at the time.

He was equally unacademic when faced with the
dispute between the trade unions, demanding that
highly paid Jewish labour must replace Arabs in the
citrus groves, and the orange growers, unwilling to
sacrifice their profits to Socialist ideology. Here, once
again, he judged the problem by the single standard:
which solution will help to build a Jewish nation?
He saw that if Jews were to be persuaded to accept
the harsh life of the countryside, they could not be
degraded to the standard of the Arab land worker.
Hence his readiness to back Ben-Gurion and other
labour leaders who preached the doctrine that, what-

ever the cost, the State of Israel must be based not
on Arab fellahin but on Jewish manual labour; not
on an impoverished peasantry but on a free trade
union of agricultural workers. For Ben-Gurion and
his colleagues in the Histadrut, this mystique was
the core of their Zionism. For Weizmann it was only
one of the many motifs to be used in inspiring Jews
to build the Jewish state. Hence his comfortable certainty that when the era of pioneering was over and
prosperity achieved, everyone would be glad to see
the austerity and severity of the collective settlements
disappear.

On this point Weizmann's pragmatism sometimes
brought him very near to an acceptance of the
"white-settler" mentality that has had such disastrous effects in Kenya and Algeria. As a Socialist,
Ben-Gurion saw that what was basically wrong with
the white settler in Africa was his refusal to do
menial tasks and his determination to be an over-
seer, not a worker. The greatest contribution, indeed,
of Ben-Gurion and his colleagues at this period was
their refusal to accept the rather complacent bourgeois standards of material comfort which Weizmann too easily assumed to be universal. One cannot inspire the kind of devotion required to found
a *kibbutz* on a desolate hillside in Galilee or in the
tropical heat of the Jordan valley by the kind of
tolerant scepticism which Weizmann displayed towards the earnest doctrinal wrangles of the *kib-
butznik*. But it is to Weizmann's credit that although
he could not resist laughing at the hair-shirt puri-

33

tanism of these earnest Socialists, he saw that they were doing an essential job and always backed them against their critics.

Where Weizmann ceased to be either radical or even sceptical was in his attitude to the British Empire. Here the critical, questing mind, ready to consider every proposal, however extreme, was disconcertingly acquiescent. Weizmann accepted almost without question the virtues of the Empire and assumed that one of the tasks of the Jewish nation would be to protect Britain's imperial interests on the Suez Canal. Only the hard and bitter events of the nineteen-thirties drove him, against his deepest inclination, into opposition to Britain.

The key to this apparent contradiction lies, once again, in Weizmann's pragmatic statesmanship. In that schoolboy letter at the age of eleven, he had argued that the Jews must have the protection of a great power. Now he added, "Whatever revolutionary methods I adopt in getting the Jews into Palestine, I can't do it without the support of Great Britain. And if I want British support, I've got to win the confidence of the British government. I've got to take the ruling class at its face value. I've got to put the best interpretation on everything it says. Because if I don't, where am I?" In retrospect, this attitude may be condemned as opportunist. But I believe it was the only conceivable way, first, of obtaining the Balfour Declaration from the wartime coalition and then, after the war, of persuading a reluctant British government to accept the Mandate

and create a British protectorate for the embryonic
Jewish state.

IX

The fact that he refused to criticise British imperial policy did not mean that Weizmann was
blind to the difficulties and the dangers of relying
on British Governments. On the contrary, he showed
remarkable foresight in anticipating the problems
which the Mandate would bring. Here, for example,
is a letter which Weizmann wrote but never sent
to Winston Churchill. After he had finished it he
was advised it was better not to write quite so frankly
to an Englishman. So there it lies in the Rehovoth
Archives, unsent and, until now, unpublished. The
date is July, 1921, six weeks after the May pogrom—
the first of the troubles which were to destroy the
Mandate. An Arab delegation was about to arrive in
London and Weizmann was anxious lest the Colonial Secretary should succumb to the pressure of his
officials and repudiate the Balfour Declaration. The
whole letter is too long to reproduce, but here are
the most arresting passages:

DEAR MR. CHURCHILL,
. . . I should not be writing to you now if I did
not believe that there was a natural alliance, almost
an identity of interest, between Zionism and England in Palestine. . . . On the other hand, there

are some amongst us who are beginning to reproach me for what I think you will count as a
virtue in a British subject. They say: "The alliance
with Great Britain on which you lean is piercing
your hand. Great Britain used Zionism to confirm
the position won in Palestine by its arms; but, that
moral position won, it now scorns the degrees by
which it ascended to it, and is about to throw you
and your ladder down." This sort of reproach
touches in a very sore place, for I have regretfully
to admit that recent British policy in Palestine has
been disappointing. . . .

The best beginning of my complaint against
present policy in Palestine is in the speech of Sir
Herbert Samuel on June 3rd of this year. What the
Balfour promise meant, Sir Herbert said, was that
some among the Jews, "within the limits that are
fixed by the numbers and interests of the present
population, should come to Palestine in order to
help by their resources and efforts to develop the
country to the advantage of all its inhabitants." I
can attach no meaning to these words but this, that
the Jewish National Home of the war-promise has
now in peace-time been transformed into an Arab
national home. . . .

And, as though this injury were not enough in
itself, its hurt is increased by the occasion on which
it is inflicted. I do not want to exaggerate the
stories of Arab outrages on Jews, but I have always
desired that as little as possible should be said about
them. After all, things just as bad occur in Egypt

and India, and nothing is said. What is peculiar to Palestine is that these outrages should actually be used as propaganda against the victims and that Jews in Palestine should be beaten, as it were, with their own crutches. I cannot understand it except in the theory of an anti-Zionist kink in some official minds. Jews who came to Palestine on the strength of a British promise and a Mandate, are made the objects of brutal attacks by the Arabs, and the Government intends to propitiate the Arabs, prohibits the immigration of Jews for a season, and whittles down the Balfour promise to nothing. . . . I have been blamed for saying that what we want is a state in Palestine that is Jewish, as England is English. I will so far amend that as to say that we want a Palestine that is Jewish in the sense that Great Britain is English, but that is the irreducible bedrock of our demands. It is not perhaps so much the fault of the High Commissioner having made his speech on June 3rd. The trouble lies deeper (if I may say so). The conditions for his becoming an effectual managing trustee of the British and Zionist interests have not been created. He was given the trust estate with encumbrances which tied the hands of Sir Herbert Samuel or of anyone not endowed with more than ordinary strength and resolution.

Let me explain in more detail what these encumbrances were. The first was a very imperfect sympathy between the military administration and the Zionists. . . . The same insubordination (if I

may so call it) was reproduced in the civil administration. You yourself have said that nine-tenths of
the officials in Palestine are completely out of sympathy with Zionism. Whose fault was that? . . .
The Government thought that they had done their
whole duty by appointing Sir Herbert Samuel.
But even if he had been stronger than he is, he
would still have been powerless to discharge his
duty with nine-tenths of his officials opposed to
Zionism. We are reproached for not establishing
better relations with the Arabs of Palestine. How
was that possible with the balance between us
oscillating and with the Government on the Hill
speaking one policy and the Government in the
Plain acting another? This oscillation was an invitation to the Arabs to be restive in the hope that
they might further disturb the balance in their
own favour. They were not discouraged in Palestine; they have even been encouraged by prominent men in England and in Palestine in their
policy of opposition and obstruction. A hero at
Government House might perhaps have established equilibrium. But I cannot bring myself to
censure Sir Herbert Samuel for not being a superman and carrying off the gates of Gaza on his own
back. I realise only too acutely how manifold and
world-wide the distractions of the Government
have been. Since the peace, devolution of a sort
may well have seemed the only way out; but this
devolution was on a foundation of sand.

Sir Herbert Samuel's encumbrances became

greater, for presently he found himself hampered too by the anti-waste agitation and by the traditional doubts of Liberalism over anything that might by any stretch of the imagination seem to savour of Imperial adventure. . . . On the accusation of waste, may I be allowed to offer some considerations? It is a charge that I feel very keenly because the vulgar idea of Jews is that they are all millionaires and the suggestion that they are battening on the poor British taxpayer is very damaging. Believe me, the chief support to Zionism comes not from the rich but from the poor Jews who in many cases, by stinting their bodily wants, sustain their ages-old ideal. . . .

The answer to the charge of waste is threefold. The stock objection to the acquisition of new responsibilities is the speculative character of the economic development, the doubt whether there are the makings in the new country of a state that can stand by itself, and the fear of military commitments. In all these regards the situation in Palestine is exceptionally favourable. You are assured of the influx of a people in which patriotism is already formed and who would feel themselves under a deep obligation to you. You are working with an organisation which is prepared to take a great deal of the financial responsibility for the upbuilding of the country, and finally, if it is the cost of the garrison that appears too high, you could solve it, supposing that all else failed and you cared for that solution, by arming and organising the Jewish colonists. Was a colonisation ever conducted under such favourable conditions . . . ?

Secondly, if there were no Palestine it would, I believe, be necessary to create one in the Imperial interest. It is a bastion to Egypt. On the one side, the existence of a Jewish Palestine leaves you absolutely free to follow whatever policy may be most convenient to you, and enables you, if you wished, to evacuate Egypt altogether and to concentrate in the Canal Zone with your army based on Palestine. The real defence of Egypt against foreign enemies is at sea and on land in Palestine, and if one was paying three times as much on the military garrison of Palestine one would be purchasing these strategic advantages very cheaply.

Lastly, you have set up a great Arab kingdom in Mesopotamia, but for all that, you will have to rely in Palestine on the Jews for your loyal element. . . . It is difficult to understand how one can build on Arab loyalty so near the vital communications across the Isthmus of Suez. All one has seen and heard of the Arab movement leads one to believe that it is anti-European.

The Palestine-Zionist policy, far from being waste, becomes a necessary insurance that we quote to you at a lower rate than anyone else could dream of. . . .

I write to beg of you not to throw away the substance for the shadow of strength, not to buy temporary accommodation at the cost of permanent accession of strength and it might be (if the promise were not kept) at the price of honour, and, finally, to take a lesson from the Turks, who maintained order in Palestine with three men and a boy. Why? Because they knew their own minds, miserable as they were, and never suffered an ambiguity to infect their policy. You can do the same if you know your own minds and act on the awe that your settled will inspires everywhere in the world. . . .*

This letter proves that Weizmann was not, as some of his adversaries pretended, without comprehension of British weaknesses. He understood Britain better than some of his critics, but he also knew that he had to trust us and acquiesce in our imperial policies. This involved an inconsistency in his values and a quite artificial division in his mind between the Jewish area, where he was critical and radical, and the British area, where he was conservative and acquiescent. But the fact is that only a man capable of this inconsistency could have obtained the Balfour Declaration.

X

So we come to the last feature of the false Weizmann legend that needs exploding, the accusation that he was Anglicised and that the attraction he exerted in London was the result of his acquired

* For full text see Appendix A.

British tastes and attitudes. The truth is the precise opposite. The attraction of Weizmann for the British was precisely that he was the most Jewish Jew we had met. He impressed us *because* he was not Western, *because* he was not assimilated, *because* he was utterly proud to be a Russian Jew from the Pale, *because* he had no feeling of double loyalty, *because* he knew only one patriotism, the love of a country that did not yet exist.

There remains the charge that Weizmann was pro-British. If by this is meant that he subordinated the establishment of the Jewish state to the interests of the British Empire, I regard the accusation as completely unfounded. Indeed, most of our Arabists assert the precise opposite—that this crafty Jew persuaded Balfour, Milner and Lloyd George to subordinate Britain's imperial interests to a Jewish cause which endangered Britain's whole Middle Eastern position. Yet this does not dispose of the whole indictment. Weizmann, as we have seen, was enamoured of Britain, particularly of the British ruling class, by which, after 1917, for a period at least, he was treated as something of a lion. It is never easy to dislike people who are enraptured by your personality, and when this unknown Jew from Motol found that Balfour, Milner, Lloyd George, Salisbury and many other great and mighty rulers of the British Empire had fallen under his spell, he not unnaturally regarded them as good people, who were basically to be trusted. Nevertheless, it is not my impression that in any of his countless diplomatic dealings with successive Governments Weizmann let the British off lightly. Particularly in the nineteen-thirties, lesser men might have given up hope of persuading either the officials or the politicians to fulfill a promise whose consequences were in such stark contrast to those expected. I can think of no occasion on which Weizmann was guilty of appeasement in his relations with Britain. If he yielded, as he frequently did, to *force majeure,* he did so only after having ensured, by extremely competent lobbying, the maximum parliamentary obstruction! No man knew better than he the art of using the conscience and ambition of British politicians (including, perhaps, the author of this book) in the interests of the Jewish state.

A personal anecdote will help to illustrate this point. In 1948, during the last phase of the war of independence, I was staying at Rehovoth with Weizmann, and a large reception was given in my honour. At one point a gushing woman pushed towards me and said, "I must introduce our Commander-in-Chief, Yigael Yadin, to our pro-Jewish guest, Mr. Crossman." For the first time I looked into the big, quizzical eyes of the archaeologist turned soldier and wondered what he would say. "Mr. Crossman is not pro-Jewish," he remarked, "but pro-British. After all, he was the prime author of the Anglo-American Commission's report, and I remember that when we were discussing our attitude to it, Dr. Weizmann remarked on the ruthlessness of some English politicians. 'This report,' he told us

43

angrily, 'was nicely calculated to concede the minimum to the Jews in order to obtain their acquiescence.'" I can remember that the throng around me seemed to melt uncomfortably away and I was left with Yadin smiling at me and, behind him, the sardonic face of Weizmann, who had overheard the conversation.

What is true, however, is that Weizmann increasingly believed in the mutual value of the Anglo-Jewish association. There is no evidence that any such idea had entered his head either when he arrived in England or in 1906, during his first talk to Balfour. At that time he was appealing purely and simply to British generosity. But during the negotiations before the Balfour Declaration there began to develop in his mind a sense that destiny had united the fate of the British and the Jewish people. And this article of faith was then confirmed by all kinds of strategic and economic arguments. We have already seen in the draft of the letter which he never sent to Winston Churchill an illustration of this aspect of Weizmann's Zionism. As the new settlers began to pour in, his conviction grew that Britain needed a reliable democratic ally in the Middle East and that only a Jewish community, rooted in the soil of its ancient homeland, could provide it.

But the most powerful argument in Weizmann's mind for the British connection was that any other connection would have been far worse for the Jews. No one could deny that the creation of a National Home required the protection of a great power. And if that great power were not Britain, who else was available? At one time, before President Wilson had been repudiated by Congress, there seemed to be a chance that the Americans would consent to hold the Mandate. Weizmann was always opposed to the idea, and the troubles of 1945 to 1948 never shook this view. I remember discussing with him the appalling incident when two British sergeants, who had been taken as hostages, were hanged in reprisal for the execution of two Irgun terrorists. What made the Irgun's revenge more terrible was the attachment of a booby trap to the body of one of the sergeants, which killed one of the men who tried to cut it down. The photograph on the front page of most of the popular British newspapers on the day after the crime was one of the most terrible I have ever seen. Weizmann's comment was characteristic. "If the sergeants had been American and not British," he observed to me, "we should have had pogroms in New York and Chicago. Bevin may be terrible, but the American Army would have behaved far worse than yours."

I shall have something more to say on this theme in my second chapter. Here, I am only concerned to analyse the character and extent of Weizmann's pro-Britishness. It contained three elements: First, a rational recognition that since Britain was the Mandatory, any responsible Jewish leader must conform the development of the National Home to British requirements, at least until it was strong enough to fend for itself. Secondly, a gratitude to the country which had accepted him as a foreigner and the liberalism of whose ruling classes he savoured with especial pleasure. Thirdly, an instinct, first felt by the schoolboy and later fully developed by the statesman, that the destinies of the two peoples were linked together, in the sense that they required the same kind of world and the same kind of balance of power in order to secure their freedom.

Was this view shared by British politicians? Probably, in the case of the authors of the Balfour Declaration, the answer is yes. But as soon as the difficulties began to multiply in the nineteen-twenties, the sense of a common destiny rapidly weakened on the British side and was finally transformed, in the case of Attlee and Bevin, into a bitter conviction that the creation of a Jewish state would imperil Britain's imperial communications and oil supplies. Only a handful of British politicians remained faithful to the vision once shared with Weizmann.

It is against this background that we can measure his real achievement. His role was not that of the courtier-diplomat, paring down the claims of his small people in order to suit the imperial requirements of Britain. On the contrary, his achievement was to charm three British statesmen out of their usual concentration on national self-interest and persuade them to take a great risk for the sake of a good cause. This is not something the British have done very often in their history. That we did it in 1917 was due to the personality of a Russian-Jewish chemist who outargued Milner and outcharmed

46

Lloyd George and Balfour. In wartime, at the height of their power, they looked into the tragic eyes of this Jew and felt their consciences stirred. Then, just when the tension was becoming a little un-British, they found themselves laughing—because the next facet of Weizmann's character was his humour, the most intensely Jewish I have ever experienced. And after that came the third transformation. The tragic Jew, the sardonic humourist, within a minute had been transformed into a scientist, cooling his listeners off with a douche of sparkling analysis. No wonder few British politicians could resist him.

Here, indeed, is one of the very rare cases where one can assert with confidence that one man's personality changed the course of history. Without the personality of Weizmann there would have been no Balfour Declaration and no Mandate. There would have been only the slow, painful kind of build-up of Jewish life in Zion which had preceded World War I. And this might well have been extinguished in the nineteen-thirties by the convulsions of Arab nationalism, with which I shall be dealing in my second chapter.

But one question remained. After the Balfour Declaration had been signed and after the Mandate had been set up, how long would the spell hold? You can charm the British out of their national egotism for a certain time. But would the charm last until the Yishuv* had grown strong enough to

* The Hebrew word for the Jewish population of Palestine.

47

fend for itself? The supreme justification of Weizmann as a Jewish statesman is that the spell he cast
gave the Yishuv just enough time. When it failed,
his own people had grown up to the point where
they were strong enough to disown him as pro-
British and accept as leaders men fitted not to charm
the British but to get rid of them.

II

The End of the Mandate

ERNEST BEVIN

Aʟᴛʜᴏᴜɢʜ it was wound up only twelve years ago, the British Mandate in Palestine is already ancient history—or rather, to be more exact, it belongs to the prehistory of the State of Israel. Those of us who took part in the turbulent politics of that time can see our roles examined by historians who belong to well-established conflicting traditions. For an orthodox British historical interpretation is already emerging which treats the Balfour Declaration as a misguided act of imperial generosity, bound from the first to end in ruin and disaster. An excellent example of this British view has been presented to us recently by Mr. John Marlowe in his *The Seat of Pilate*. Mr. Marlowe concludes what must be the first complete history of the Mandate with a judgment that falls with equal severity on Lord Balfour and Mr. Bevin.

One of the hills on which Jerusalem is built is called The Mount of Evil Counsel. The spirit of this hill seems to have brooded over the British adventure in Palestine. At the beginning the attempt to use Zionism as an instrument of British policy was prompted by evil counsel. At the end the attempt to use Arab nationalism as an instrument of British policy was equally prompted by evil counsel. But always this evil counsel, whispered to Balfour in 1917 and to Bevin in 1947, seemed invested with the irresistible cogency conferred by the unconscious obsessions of the men who uttered it. For the British failed in Palestine not as a result of too little imagination on the part of their administrators but as the result of too much imagination on the part of their advisers. The dream of a Levant regenerated by Jewish enterprise was as chimerical as the vision of an Arab Confederation westernized by British "know-how." *

Particularly in the United States and in Israel, another and quite different interpretation of the Mandate is gaining currency. This holds that, so far from being chimerical, the Balfour Declaration was an act of real statesmanship, which was betrayed by successive British Governments and High Commissioners. Britain's pledge to the Jews could have been fulfilled and an independent Israeli state could have developed peacefully out of the National Home if Britain had conducted her Middle Eastern policy on sound lines and carried out the terms of the Mandate without prejudice against the Jews.

* John Marlowe, *The Seat of Pilate* (London, Cresset Press, 1959), pp. 252-253. By permission of the publishers.

I

Is either of these two versions of history correct? In order to find an answer to this question, I shall first summarise the case against the administration of the Mandate, which I suspect is rapidly becoming the orthodox version of Israeli prehistory outside Britain. This indictment has four heads. First, that the military administration was violently anti-Jewish; secondly, that the civil administration was composed of colonial officials, many of them from the African colonies and imbued with the philosophy of protecting the native against the "white settler"; thirdly, that the politicians at Westminster were chronically weak; and, fourthly, that the Jews were finally sacrificed in an attempt to appease the Arabs, so that they should not fall under the influence first of the Nazis and Fascists and then, after 1945, of the Soviet Union. There is substance in every charge. But I do not believe that they add up to a proof that the whole project was "chimerical."

Take, for instance, the criticisms of the colonial officials. At the end of that letter to Churchill which he never sent, Weizmann insisted on the necessity for purging the administration of "every insubordinate who will not work for the Mandate." What a brilliant phrase! For the story of Palestine from 1921 to 1948 is, indeed, the history of insubordinates who frequently refused to carry the Mandate out. This kind of administrative indiscipline is most unusual in British colonial history. One reason for it, certainly, was the fact that, with the exception of India and the Sudan, which had their own special services, colonial officials were normally moved at short intervals from one colony to another. Between colonies of the same type, this did not matter. In most of our African colonies and dependencies, for example, one of the main tasks of the colonial official was to protect the backward native population against exploitation by more civilised colonists, whether white or Indian. A deeply conscientious official, steeped in this tradition of paternal trusteeship, sometimes found it difficult to adjust himself when he was suddenly transferred from the Gold Coast to Cyprus or from Tanganyika to Palestine, where he had to deal with Cypriote Greeks or Palestinian Jews, who neither were nor felt themselves culturally inferior.

This was impressed upon me some years ago on my first visit to Cyprus, when the present Governor of Nyasaland, Sir Robert Armitage, was still in charge. He was in the true tradition of the Palestine High Commissioners. When I first went to see him, I noticed on his desk a photograph of Dr. Nkrumah, and he said to me, "Nkrumah's an old friend of mine. I was Financial Secretary on the Gold Coast before I came here." A few minutes later we were talking about Cyprus and I said, "Have you any trouble with the Greeks about Enosis?" to which he replied, "If they really wanted it we would have had trouble long ago, such as we had in Palestine."

"Isn't it rather dangerous to talk like that?" I enquired. "Oh, no, I always talk to them quite straight and tell them that if only they would follow the example of Nkrumah, they might come as fast as he has towards independence." "But surely," I said, "Nkrumah was gaoled as a Communist and was taken straight out of gaol to become Prime Minister! Is that the example you want the Cypriotes to follow?"

From that moment, I am afraid that Sir Robert Armitage classified me among the "awkwards," in just the same way as the British officials in Palestine had done when I interrogated them as a member of the Anglo-American Commission. My crime had been to analyse Sir Robert's policies logically, and this was a failing I shared with the Palestine Jews. One of the things which made the officials who administered the Mandate anti-Jewish was the fact that the Jews are logical people who studied the facts and were not afraid to prove that a British official was talking nonsense. To the average colonial administrator this kind of objectivity was distasteful and he tended to prefer "natives" to people who treated him as an equal and could argue his head off. He found it difficult to be impartial between an Arab, to whom he could feel paternally superior, and a Jew, who made him feel uncomfortable all through the interview.

In the case of the British Army and the Palestine police, the anti-Jewish bias was stronger and simpler. As Weizmann himself pointed out, when Palestine was first occupied in 1917, nine-tenths of the officers were anti-Zionist and a high proportion of them were anti-Semitic as well. Throughout the Mandate the average British soldier and policeman, very soon after his arrival in Palestine, became pro-Arab and anti-Jew. As for the tiny minority who evinced Zionist convictions, one could usually trace their eccentricity to a female connection—and this was especially true of the Palestine police. If a soldier or policeman didn't have a Jewish girl, he was nearly always on the side of the "poor old Arab."

It is becoming fashionable—especially among Israelis who claim to be "activists"—to blame Weizmann in particular for tolerating and forgiving this anti-Jewish bias in the British Army and the British colonial service. My comment on this criticism is that if it was a sin for a Jew to forgive the British, then Weizmann shared the sin with hundreds of thousands of other Israelis. One of the most remarkable experiences of an Englishman who visits Israel today is the discovery that the "forgive-and-forget" attitude which characterised Weizmann has now spread to almost the whole population. Reminiscing about the Mandate consumes almost as much time in Israel as storytelling about "the Troubles" in southern Ireland. Yet what a difference there is in the attitude of the Irish towards their British oppressors! In Tipperary, for example, you will not often hear an Irishman say, "Well, after all, thank God it was the English! If we had to go through it with any oppressor, we'd rather it was you." But there can be few Englishmen who have not had this said to them during their travels in Israel.

When I was travelling through Galilee recently I spent the evening with the Mayor of Safad and a group of young men, all of whom had been active members of the Haganah. What tales they had to tell of that pleasant British trick which consisted of handing over any police station in a dominating position, from which the Jews could easily be exterminated, to the Arabs! This occurred in many parts of the country, but Safad is perhaps the most dramatic example of a cool, calculated attempt to ensure that the Jews would perish at the hands of the Arabs. These stories led us on to discuss the corruption of the Palestine police and the savage methods they employed in conducting their investigations. One of the stories was so terrible that I exclaimed, "When I hear about the behaviour of our men, I really begin to feel some sympathy with the Irgun." At once there was a frigid silence in the room. *"Cha,"* said one young man, "but we strongly disapproved of that kind of thing. We fought a clean fight against a clean enemy." "But surely that's ridiculous! In war you can't be so choosy," I said, to which I got the reply, "But we weren't making war. We didn't want to get rid of you. We wanted the British to work with us."

I believe that this conversation reveals an important and astonishing aspect of Anglo-Jewish relations. Unlike the Irish, who really wanted to get rid of us in Ireland, the Yishuv, or a very large part of it, was content with the British connection. They saw the growth of the National Home as something perfectly compatible with continued British protection and permanent membership of the British Commonwealth. Weizmann was not the only member of the Yishuv who preached "organic" Zionism, who passionately wanted co-operation with Britain, who would have made great concessions in order to achieve it, and who, after the rupture of 1948, said, "Now, thank God, we can live on friendly terms." It is fair enough to recall the shortcomings of the Army, the colonial officials and the Palestine police, but we can now see how superficial were the wounds in Anglo-Jewish relations caused by those shortcomings. No! The Mandate did not founder because of the flaws in the British administration, and there are few Israelis who would now deny that the benefits bestowed by the British colonial officials and the British Army on the embryonic nation were infinitely greater than the wounds they inflicted.

Let us turn, then, to the last two charges of the indictment—the indecision at Westminster and the policy of appeasement. No man told the story with more merciless incisiveness than Weizmann. Here is a letter which he wrote to Mr. Ormsby-Gore, later Lord Harlech, when he was Colonial Secretary in 1938.

What was the record? Complete inaction; paralysis of Government; surrender to Crown; demoralisation of the Civil Service; men willing and able

58

to do their duty prevented by the faint-heartedness
of superiors; denial of justice; failure to protect the
lives and property of law-abiding citizens; in short
a condition of things unthinkable in any other
part of the British Empire. These things fall to a
great extent into your term of office. In vain did
we appeal to you to see authority re-established in
Palestine. . . . You, Mr. Ormsby-Gore, closed your
letter by urging me not to burn my boats, not to
go off the deep end. I have no boats to burn. You
further asked me not to come up with a flourish of
trumpets. Can you in the last year point to a single
occasion on which I have done so? I have borne
most things in silence. I have defended the British
administration before my own people on public
platforms, at Congresses, in all parts of the world,
often against my better knowledge, and almost
invariably to my own detriment. Why did I do so?
Because for me close co-operation with Great
Britain was the corner-stone of our policy in
Palestine, but the co-operation remained unilateral.
It was unrequited.

Once again the charge is substantially true. Palestine is a blemish on the record of Conservative
statesmen in the nineteen-thirties and of Labour
statesmen in the nineteen-forties. But sufficient time
has now elapsed to enable us to start examining this
sorry record with historical detachment. We can now
ask what made British politicians behave in this
extraordinary way—a way which most Israelis now

feel to be uncharacteristic and un-British. What drove them to it? What made them mad?

II

Those of us who are too young to have been politically conscious in 1917 must use our imagination in order to breathe again the climate of that year. In 1917 not only Lloyd George, Balfour and Milner but virtually the whole of thinking public opinion in Britain saw no moral objection at all to taking over a backward slice of the Turkish Empire and permitting the Jews to pour into it until they had achieved their majority. Weizmann was assured by friends in Whitehall that if you looked through the Foreign Office papers, you would find that none of the Arabist objections were made *before* the Balfour Declaration was launched. Colonel Lawrence, for example, who ten years later felt bitterly that the Arabs had been betrayed, in 1917 accepted the idea of the National Home and failed to predict that Arab nationalism would passionately oppose it.

What a contrast with the political climate when I first concerned myself with the Palestine problem! I arrived in Jerusalem straight from Dachau, quite overwhelmed by the need of European Jewry to return home. After travelling across Germany and Austria in the winter of 1945, I did not need to be taught the Jewish case. I knew it *by* heart and *from* the heart. And yet, directly I arrived in Jerusalem,

I was forced into an agonising reappraisal. What stuck in my gullet was the idea that British troops should be used to hold the Arabs down while the Jews were given time to create an artificial Jewish majority. Sure enough, I did at last come to the conclusion that the injustice done to the Arabs by dividing the country and permitting the Jews to achieve a majority in their portion would be less than the injustice done to the Jews by implementing the 1938 White Paper. But this was a complicated, terribly difficult decision to reach.

What was it, after World War I, that completely changed the moral basis of the Palestine problem? In 1917 not only British statesmen but King Feisal as well found no difficulty in accepting the National Home. Yet before the nineteen-twenties were over, no fair-minded person could deny that in the process of building the Jewish state a grave injustice would be done to the Arabs. By the middle of the nineteen-thirties the clash of Jewish and Arab nationalism had made the Mandate entirely unworkable, and when I arrived in Jerusalem just after World War II, the choice seemed to me to lie between partition imposed by the British Army and partition carved out by the Haganah after a British withdrawal. What had gone wrong? What were the new destructive elements in the situation which were not foreseen either by Chaim Weizmann or by Arthur Balfour?

The tragedy of Palestine arose from the fact that a new historical epoch began between 1917 and 1922.

In those crucial five years between the Balfour Declaration and the Mandate, there occurred two events which heralded the end of European world domination and the beginning of the period in which Europe is merely one province of world politics among others. The instruments which effected this change were the two secret weapons employed during the First World War, one by the Germans and the other by ourselves. The first secret weapon was the decision of Ludendorff to send Lenin in the sealed train from Switzerland to Russia and so make possible the establishment of the first Communist state. The revolutionary philosophy used by Ludendorff in order to disintegrate the morale of the Russian Army was turned against the West by Lenin and Trotsky when they seized power. And once the lifeline of the British Empire was threatened by a revolutionary Communist state to the north, British Governments were bound to reassess the value to them of the Jewish National Home.

The second secret weapon was the doctrine of "national self-determination," associated with the name of Woodrow Wilson. It was employed by the psychological warriors of World War I in order to disrupt the Austro-Hungarian Empire. As an ex-psychological warrior, I observe that our predecessors in the First World War were allowed to do things forbidden to us in the second! We were strictly limited to propaganda and forbidden to suggest policies which, for example, would have exploited the fall of Mussolini in 1943 or the German generals'

Putsch twelve months later. Our predecessors, on the other hand, were permitted to evolve policies which broke up the German alliance. Once the Czechs, the Poles, the Hungarians and the other small nations of Central Europe had been promised self-determination and assured that every oppressed nation would be permitted to achieve sovereignty, the defeat of the Germans was certain. At the time, national self-determination was thought of as a fine instrument for breaking up the Pan-German Empire, but within a few years it was proving equally efficacious as a weapon for destroying the British and French Empires. From 1920 onwards, these two weapons—national self-determination and revolutionary Communism—began to corrode the European colonial empires.

Those who denounce the folly of the authors of the Balfour Declaration surely forget that these two forces emerged *after* it was proclaimed. What made it unworkable was the fact that world Jewry began to return to Zion, in the very decade when the colonial peoples were, for the first time, challenging European world domination.

III

The classic pattern for colonial revolution was established, ironically enough, by a European people, the Irish. The first of the terrorists, partisans or lead-

63

ers of resistance—whichever you like to call them—
was Mr. de Valera. In many previous wars, civilians
had resisted uniformed armies, but no one had
glorified them as guerrillas and revolutionaries.
World opinion still regarded war as a matter for
professionals. De Valera got rid of the British by
encouraging Irish civilians to shoot British soldiers
in the back and to burn them alive in the houses
where they were sleeping. He won because world
public opinion was more shocked by British oppression than it was by Irish atrocities.

I learnt the importance of the Irish revolution in
modern history in the course of my first long private
talk with Gamal Nasser, then Neguib's Chief of
Staff and virtually unknown. Checking with my
diary, I find the date was December, 1953. I was
taken to see him at a private house in Cairo and told
that he was the man who had really organised the
Egyptian revolution. One of the first questions I
asked him was what books he read.

"What do you mean, books?"

"Well, you know, books about revolutions." In
my mind books and revolutions are connected. They
were not in his.

"Do you mean manuals of military training?"

"No. Karl Marx."

"Marx? I don't read Marx. I'm not a Communist!"

"Well, do you read democratic books?"

"What is a democratic book?"

I said, rather desperately, "Harold Laski," to
which I got the expected reply, "Who is he?" So

64

then I said, "Well, have you ever read a book about politics?"

"Yes, I've read one. It's called *Grey Wolf*. It's an Englishman's account of Kemal Atatürk and how he achieved national liberation and national unity for his people. That is the most important book in my life. Only I can't ever play the role of Atatürk here in Egypt, because we Egyptians are free Western people and not primitive barbarians like the Turks."

"In that case, how will you achieve it?"

"Ah," he said, "I remember now. I have read another book. I have forgotten its name, but it told me exactly how the Irish threw the British out of Ireland. That book will be the textbook of our Egyptian revolution."

Nasser is not the only nationalist to regard Ireland as the pattern. The idea of national self-determination, achieved by organising civilian resistance on the Irish pattern, has spread to the colonial world. In some cases the forces that dominate the movement are Right Wing, inspired by the ideas of national democracy. Sometimes they are Communist. And more often they are an alliance between the two.

We can now see what happened to make the Mandate almost unworkable even before it began. Both the British and Dr. Weizmann had expected that the Jews would come into Palestine and build their Western, civilised State without upsetting the less civilised "natives." What actually happened, as we all know, is that Jewish and Arab nationalism interacted on each other and the Arab intelligentsia began to regard the Middle East as the classic pattern of Leninist "imperial exploitation." If the Jewish settlers had achieved their majority before 1914, they would have been accepted without moral compunction of any kind. But now they roused the opposition not merely of the Arabs and the Arabists but of many Liberals and Socialists who also felt that they were "white settlers," like the British in Kenya or the French in Algeria.

Here again it is important to rid oneself of hindsight. For generations it had been assumed that civilisation would be spread by the white man settling overseas. The Portuguese and the Spaniards had settled South America, the French and British had settled North America, the Dutch had gone to South Africa. No one until the twentieth century seriously challenged their right, or indeed their duty, to civilise these continents by physically occupying them, even at the cost of wiping out the aboriginal population. The French settlement in North Africa and the British settlement in East and Central Africa were the last examples of a "civilising mission," which had been morally acceptable to Europeans for more than four hundred years. Then, towards the end of World War I, its morality was challenged. Of course, as we can see in Algeria as well as in Central and South Africa, there are still settlers who believe unquestioningly in the white man's burden. But in the home countries what was once self-evident

66

has become a matter of agonising reappraisal.

So the Jew was not, as Ernest Bevin once suggested, "the first in the queue," but the last. If, instead of offering Uganda in 1903, Chamberlain had been able to make the Balfour Declaration, no one would have questioned the right of the Jews to settle in Palestine, achieve a majority over the Arab inhabitants and establish a Jewish state. Twenty years later the establishment of the National Home was seen not as the return of an ancient people to their own country but as yet another episode in the cruel history of imperialism. Occurring, as it did, in the epoch of Woodrow Wilson's "national self-determination" and Lenin's Communist revolution, it was bound to arouse not only resistance in the Arab world but a profound moral malaise in the West.

The first occasion on which this aspect of Zionism was brought home to me was during the sittings of the Anglo-American Commission in Cairo. Most of the proceedings were extremely boring. But one moment stands out in my memory, the impromptu and moving speech with which Azzam Pasha, then Secretary of the Arab League, introduced his memorandum. One passage of this speech in particular sticks in my mind:

> Our brother has gone to Europe and to the West and come back something else. He has come back a Russified Jew, a Polish Jew, a German Jew, an English Jew. He has come back with a totally different conception of things, Western and not Eastern. That does not mean that we are necessarily

quarrelling with anyone who comes from the West. But the Jew, our old cousin, coming back with imperialistic ideas, with materialistic ideas, with reactionary or revolutionary ideas, and trying to implement them first by British pressure and then by American pressure, and then by terrorism on his own part—he is not the old cousin, and we do not extend to him a very good welcome. The Zionist, the new Jew, wants to dominate, and he pretends that he has got a particular civilising mission with which he returns to a backward, degenerate race in order to put the elements of progress into an area which has no progress. Well, that has been the pretension of every power that wanted to colonise and aimed at domination. The excuse has always been that the people are backward and that he has got a human mission to put them forward. . . . The Arabs simply stand and say "NO." We are not reactionary and we are not backward. Even if we are ignorant, the difference between ignorance and knowledge is ten years in school. We are a living, vitally strong nation; we are in our renaissance; we are producing as many children as any nation in the world. We still have our brains. We have a heritage of civilisation and of spiritual life. We are not going to allow ourselves to be controlled either by great nations or small nations or dispersed nations.*

* *Palestine Mission* (New York, Harper & Brothers, 1947), p. 118.

I V

But does the undeniable fact of outraged Arab resistance to Zionism confirm what I have called the orthodox British view of the Mandate? Does it prove that the vision of Balfour, Lloyd George and Milner was chimerical and that those politicians and administrators who decided to go back on our promise to the Jews were justified in the actions they took? In my view, the answer is no. How easy it would be, in private as well as in public life, if a change of circumstances which made it inconvenient to keep our pledged word justified us in repudiating the promise altogether! The truth is that throughout the period of the Mandate Britain was presented not with a choice between right and wrong but with a conflict of obligations. Weizmann was the only Jew or Arab to admit this frankly. Testifying before Commission after Commission, he reiterated that the choice in Palestine was not between right and wrong but between a greater and a lesser injustice. How often he warned successive British Governments and High Commissioners that there was no simple decision which would resolve this conflict. Instead, they would have to do something evil for the sake of a greater good.

The men who suffered most under the moral conflict Weizmann described were the officials in Palestine. For the politicians at Westminster, the Mandate was one of a number of problems to which they addressed their minds from time to time. For the offi-

cial in Jerusalem, it was his life. Some of them gave
up the struggle and adopted a one-sided pro-Jewish
or, much more frequently, pro-Arab position. Others
took refuge in the illusion of equidistant neutrality.
The first time I met this peculiar attitude was when
I was lunching in Jerusalem in 1946 with a British
Jew working for the Mandatory government. He
told me that it would be quite easy for the members
of the Anglo-American Commission to test whether
they had produced a good report. "If you do a good
job," he said, "you will find that you are detested
equally by both sides. That will be the proof of
your impartiality." The idea that an impartial decision must be detested by both sides and that justice
is a halfway house between two equal and opposite
extremes is, of course, a dangerous error. True
enough, in the administration of the Mandate, justice lay somewhere between a complete satisfaction
of the Jewish and a complete satisfaction of the Arab
demands. But there was no reason to believe that it
could be achieved by the simple device of finding
the middle point between them. The official who
adopted an attitude of equidistant neutrality was in
no way morally superior to his colleagues who had
fallen off the fence into the Jewish or the Arab camp.
For those who became pro-Jewish or pro-Arab were
at least facing the facts of the situation, while those
who remained neutral between the conflicting national forces could only do so by refusing to face the
justice of both claims. Both sides were right, and it
was as this recognition penetrated deeper and deeper

into the colonial administration that the Mandate became increasingly unworkable. For in such a situation the only sane course for a colonial power is to cut its losses and create as soon as possible the conditions for withdrawal.

V

But was there ever a chance for Britain to keep faith with the Jews and fulfill her promise without violating her obligations to the Arabs? I believe that the Balfour Declaration could have been fulfilled by building up a Jewish majority very quickly indeed. In order to make this possible, the British government would have had to appoint a first High Commissioner strong enough to purge his own staff of anti-Zionists, to disregard Arab opposition and encourage large-scale Jewish immigration. Obviously he would have had to be a Gentile, because no Jew selected by a British government could possibly commit the lesser injustice to the Arabs required to build the National Home in the nineteen-twenties. Once Sir Herbert Samuel was appointed the first High Commissioner, a radical policy of this kind was out of the question, and the only opportunity for fulfilling the Balfour Declaration had been missed.

But for this the British government was not solely to blame. World Jewry failed equally to fulfill its share of the task, the provision of half a million immigrants in the first few years. The main cause of this failure was, of course, the Bolshevik Revolution. Zionists had always assumed that Russia would provide the main source of mass immigration into Palestine. Alas, the Bolshevik Revolution fell like a safety curtain, separating the millions of Russian Jews from the outside world. If Russia, after the Revolution, had remained a democratic country, the whole situation might have been transformed. For with Russian manpower would have come Russian money as well to finance the creation of a Jewish state. But the Bolsheviks won, and Zionism became a forbidden heresy in the Soviet Union.

Yet another vital ingredient of success was lacking in 1921. Even if Providence had arranged for the appointment of a tough non-Jewish High Commissioner, as well as for the arrival of half a million Russian Jews, that would not have been sufficient without a Government in Westminster conscious of its imperial destiny and prepared to accept military obligations in order to fulfill it. Actually the Mandate was established during the postwar sag in British morale, during which public opinion reacted violently against military discipline and imperial obligations. The fall of the Lloyd George Government after the Chanak crisis showed how little Britain was prepared to accept new obligations in the Middle East and to fulfill the Balfour Declaration in the spirit in which it had been negotiated.

I conclude, therefore, that it is just theoretically possible to conceive conditions in the early nineteentwenties in which the Mandate could have been made to work without endangering Britain's whole Middle Eastern position. By the end of the decade, however, the opportunity for achieving a Jewish state under British protection had been missed finally and irrevocably. From now on, whether his sympathies lay with the Arabs or the Jews, the farsighted British official or politician would be driven to realise that it had become a vital national interest to end the Mandate.

VI

The first sign of this recognition that the Mandate could not work was the British reaction to the pogroms of 1929. As became normal in such circumstances, a Commission was duly sent to Palestine and Mr. Justice Shaw reported in 1930. Even before the report was issued, the Labour Government publicly declared its intention to suspend immigration, an intention confirmed when Sidney Webb, by now Lord Passfield, issued his notorious White Paper. This was one of the rare occasions when Chaim Weizmann's liking for the British ruling class destroyed his judgment. As soon as he had succeeded in forcing Ramsay MacDonald to withdraw the White Paper, he assumed that he had permanently defeated the British enemies of Zionism. In reality, something very different had happened. A weak minority Government, which a few months later was to split and collapse, had first surrendered to its officials in the Colonial Office and then, when this caused a political explosion, had surrendered ignominiously to an equal and opposite political pressure. What Weizmann failed to observe was that his momentary triumph over a weak Cabinet had been achieved at the cost of a rupture with the permanent officials, who count for very much more, in the long run, than any politician. Weizmann had only postponed the inevitable day when those permanent officials would get their way.

Of course, the years thus gained were invaluable. For between the withdrawal of the Passfield White Paper in 1930 and the Peel Commission in 1937 occurred the years of German-Jewish immigration, which transformed the Yishuv into a viable nation. It has often been remarked that Hitler recruited more Zionists than any Zionist leader. Certainly, without the Nazi persecution, Palestine Jewry would not have been strong enough to win its war of independence. Yet there was a price to be paid for the strengthening of Zionism by Hitler's persecution. Simultaneously, Fascism had been operating on the Arab world as well, and had transformed a democratic nationalism, limited to a small élite, into a mass movement inspired by anti-Western xenophobia. Tiny Palestine was a battlefield now of contending world forces. If the Mandate already appeared unworkable to Mr. Justice Shaw in 1930, the need to end it had become much more urgent when the Peel Commission visited the country and recommended partition.

74

In retrospect, I cannot feel quite so indignant about the Chamberlain Government's failure to implement the Peel report. In the year of Munich, Britain was incapable of displaying the energy required to create a Jewish state under the protection of the British Army. In the circumstances, the recommendations of the Peel Commission were sheerly impracticable and there was no alternative to the policy of appeasement, as formulated in the White Paper. It is not unfair to describe that White Paper as a Middle Eastern Munich, since the treatment Britain accorded to her Jewish allies in Palestine was just as shameful as that Czechoslovakia received from France. Nevertheless, it remains true that, with appeasement the order of the day in Europe, it was plainly impossible for a British government to apply an opposite policy in the Middle East.

The outbreak of war postponed the issue, and victory in 1945 created one last and quite unexpected chance to restore the record. For partition, which was impracticable in 1938, had suddenly been transformed into a workable, statesmanlike policy by the collapse of the Third Reich and the temporary but acute weakness of the Arab states. For a short time after the victory of 1945, Britain's authority in the Middle East was supreme and the Arab politicians were thoroughly cowed by the knowledge that they had backed the losing side. Here, then, was a moment when a British Government, with a huge army at its disposal, could end the Mandate honourably by enforcing the partition plan recommended in 1937.

It is fair to recall that this chance was first offered to Winston Churchill, who was in charge of the Caretaker Government before the election. But Churchill had been personally antagonised by the murder of Lord Moyne and he showed no inclination whatsoever to burn his fingers in Palestine. So the chance passed to the newly elected Labour Government, the first British government explicitly and repeatedly pledged to assist in the creation of the Jewish state. The chance was not only missed, it was rejected with violence and passion by Ernest Bevin.

VII

What is the explanation of the Labour Party's sorry record in its relations with Palestine? Those who put all the blame on one personality, Ernest Bevin, omit to notice that Mr. Bevin's behaviour had been anticipated by Sidney Webb in 1930. Indeed, it is fascinating to observe how the conduct of the Fabian intellectual, when he was Colonial Secretary, foreshadowed on a small scale the colossal failure of the working-class leader fifteen years later. In particular, the form which their anti-Jewish prejudices took was curiously alike. Browsing in the Weizmann Archives, I came, for example, on a long private note, a résumé of a talk which took place between Lord Passfield and General Smuts. When Smuts tried to persuade Lord Passfield to withdraw the White Paper, he was abruptly told, "It's very unfair that those Jews are so well represented. They have got Mr. Weizmann, whereas the poor Arabs haven't." When I read that passage, my mind clicked back to at least a dozen searing arguments which I had with Mr. Attlee and Mr. Bevin between 1946 and 1948. Like Lord Passfield, they convinced themselves that since the Jews were such clever propagandists and had so many friends, it was the duty of an impartial British statesman to treat everything they said with the gravest suspicion, while putting the most favourable interpretation on the Arab case.

Once again, in fact, we detect the prejudice in favour of the native and against the "white settler," which I attributed earlier to the colonial official. To my knowledge, the prime factor in both Mr. Attlee's and Mr. Bevin's Palestine thinking was the influence of their officials, in the Foreign Office even more than in the Colonial Office. I believe the same must have applied to Lord Passfield. The Coalition Government of 1917, the Conservative Government of 1924, even the National Government, in its first phase after 1931, contained men with knowledge and experience of the Middle East which enabled them to stand up to their officials. In dealing with this part of the world, however, Lord Passfield felt as little assurance as Mr. Attlee or Mr. Bevin. And that is why they were more susceptible to Whitehall pressure than Lord Milner, Sir Winston Churchill or Lord Lloyd.

Many Americans and Israelis believe that in his Palestine policy Ernest Bevin was motivated by anti-

77

Semitism. From personal experience I can say that this is untrue of his attitude in 1945. Like Lord Passfield, he already felt that the Jews were pushing, thrusting fellows and that fairness required he should prop up the poor Arabs against them. Moreover, the defence of the whole British Middle Eastern position against the Soviet Union seemed to require a continuation of the appeasement policy begun by Chamberlain. At first, I believe, Bevin was almost entirely under the influence of his Foreign Office and military advisers. He took their word and faithfully tried to implement their proposals by persuading the Jewish leaders to be "sensible." He would secure them full minority rights in an Arab puppet state, run by Britain. What more could a reasonable protagonist of the National Home demand of a British government in 1945?

It was when Weizmann, as well as Ben-Gurion, spurned his offer and made it clear that the Yishuv would resist a change of status by force of arms that Ernest Bevin's dislike of the Jews began dangerously to influence his policy. It was his habit, when faced by any difficult international problem, to find a solution based on his own trade-union experience in Britain. In this case his mind went back to the difficulties he had had in organising the Jews of the East End. He had been troubled by constant feuding between Jews and Catholics, and his solution had been to teach his union members that religious differences should not be permitted to undermine working-class solidarity. By a strange coincidence, Clement

Attlee also had his first experience of Jewish politics in the East End, when he lived as a social worker in an East End boys' club. As a result, both men got it firmly into their heads that the Jews of Palestine should be treated as a religious group, on a par with the Christians and the Moslems. The Arabs, in their view, had a right to national self-determination, because they were a nation. But the principle did not apply to the Jews, since they were only a religious community.

How often would I say, "But, Ernie, I've seen it for myself. The Palestine Jews have grown into a nation, and if you refuse them partition, they will fight for their lives." "No," he would reply, "there's only a Jewish religion, not a Jewish nation. And if those Jews in Palestine aren't religious, they ought not to call themselves Jews!" I could never move either him or Mr. Attlee on this point. Right to the end, they felt aggrieved because the Jews showed so little gratitude for all that Britain had done for them. On the first occasion that I spoke to Mr. Attlee, for example, after he had rejected our report, he greeted me with the words, "I'm disappointed in you, Dick. The report you have produced is grossly unfair." I was genuinely puzzled and said, "Unfair to the Jews or to the Arabs?" To this he replied crossly, "No, unfair to Britain, of course. You've let us down by giving way to the Jews and Americans."

A few months later Mr. Attlee's irritation had been transformed into a cold anger and Mr. Bevin's into a violent passion. It was the stubborn refusal of the

79

Yishuv to be grateful for his protection and to conform to the plans he had made for it that finally tipped Ernest Bevin into overt anti-Semitism. The British do not normally develop this mania except under very strong provocation. Ernest Bevin felt himself unbearably provoked when the Jews wantonly rejected his solution of their problem. The provocation grew when he discovered that the Russians were exploiting the issue against him and, even worse, that the Americans were ganging up with the Russians. Driven by a frightening mixture of anger and violent self-pity, he became convinced that the Jews were organising a world conspiracy against poor old Britain and, in particular, against poor old Ernie.

Of course, there were plenty of sound reasons why any British Foreign Secretary at this time would have been angry with Mr. Truman. Safe on the sidelines, the American President was urging that a hundred thousand Jews should be admitted to Palestine but was flagrantly unwilling either to send any American troops to help keep order or to relieve the pressure by permitting the survivors of the gas chambers to come to the States. Ernest Bevin, however, convinced himself that the American concern for the National Home was completely hypocritical, and publicly accused Mr. Truman of playing politics for the sake of the Jewish vote in New York. By 1947, British policy in Palestine was largely motivated by one man's determination, at almost any cost, to teach the Jews a lesson. At this stage it is difficult to deny that Mr. Bevin's usually shrewd and farsighted appreciation of any situation he was handling had become heavily clouded by anti-Semitism. One sign of this was an extraordinary credulity. One day he came and sat down beside me in the House of Commons (throughout the crisis he was always ready to talk to me, I think because he quite liked a little opposition as long as he was certain he could smash it). "Now I've got something which may finally convince you that you're in the wrong," he started. "The Foreign Office have given me their latest information from the Soviet Union. The Russians have massed an army of Jews at Odessa, ready for the attack!"

I tried to convince him that it was just *because* the leaders of the Yishuv were of Russian origin that nearly all of them were fanatically opposed to Russian Communism. Moreover, apart from a minority of fellow-travellers, I added, the leadership of the Histadrut, including David Ben-Gurion, felt that the one labour movement in the world whose ideals they shared was the British. But nothing could shake his *idée fixe* that the British position in the Middle East was threatened by a Jewish-Communist conspiracy, to which the Americans, for cynical reasons of internal politics, were giving their support.

In addition to the anti-Jewish delusions that clouded his mind, Mr. Bevin was possessed by the belief that the Arabs were a simple, straightforward people with a deep liking for the British and respect for their leadership. These illusions were systematically fed both by his Foreign Office advisers and by a flow of fantastic misinformation, which was poured onto his desk from Middle Eastern Headquarters in Egypt. One of the strangest facets of the Palestine tragedy was the skill with which first Middle Eastern Headquarters and then the Chiefs of Staff in London managed to prevent the Labour Government from receiving the military appreciation of the soldiers actually operating in Palestine. As a member of the Anglo-American Commission, I had spent a morning listening to the General Officer Commanding and cross-examining him after his formal statement. Significantly enough, this was the only evidence proffered to us which was struck from our record as too secret to be recorded. Hence I was never able to present it to Mr. Attlee or Mr. Bevin. The G.O.C. was quite explicit that the Haganah would be able without difficulty to hold any area allocated to the Jews under partition, whereas large British reinforcements would be required to police any pro-Arab solution which involved the suppression of the Haganah. Deeply impressed by this testimony, we unanimously agreed on an interim solution, just—but only just—acceptable to the Jews. The Labour Government, however, rejected the report of our Commission before the British members had even returned to London, and I was later to learn that their main reason for doing so was the advice proffered to them by the Chiefs of Staff that it would require two extra divisions to implement it!

In measuring the personal responsibility of Ernest

Bevin for the Palestine catastrophe, it is as well to remember this systematic misinformation to which he was subjected month after month by the Foreign Office and the Service Chiefs. If he had been a weaker man, he would have followed the example of Ramsay MacDonald in 1930 and shrunk back when he saw the disastrous political effects of the policies recommended to him by his experts. But Ernest Bevin was the last man to be deflected by political considerations from a course of action on which he had staked his personal prestige. He took full responsibility for the successive schemes which his experts hatched in order first to turn Palestine into an Arab state with a Jewish minority, and then, when the United Nations accepted partition and the Jewish state was born, to expose the infant to a murderous assault.

There came a time when these experts were appalled by the obsession which they had induced in the mind of their master. But by then they could not hold him. He was permitted to prosecute his vendetta until the day when five British fighters, which he had personally ordered into combat, were shot down behind the Jewish lines. I was in Palestine at the time and having tea with Weizmann when the news was announced that the fleet at Malta had been alerted. I remember Sharett's anxious question, "Will they bombard Tel Aviv?" to which I had the sense to reply, "This is *good* news, not bad. At last Bevin has overreached himself and Attlee will be forced to disown this madness." And so it turned out. With support from not a single member of the Commonwealth, Bevin could not raise the issue on the Security Council and Sir Stafford Cripps decided that things had gone far enough. In the Labour Party he formed a cabal with Mr. Herbert Morrison and, almost simultaneously, Sir Winston Churchill at last made it clear that the Conservative Opposition would, for the first time, oppose the Bevin policy in the division lobby. That was the end. Within a fortnight Britain granted *de-facto* recognition to the new state.

VIII

Must we, then, conclude that just as it was the personality of Weizmann in 1917 which was the determining factor in the achievement of the Balfour Declaration, so it was the personal prejudices of Ernest Bevin forty years later which ended the Mandate and ruptured Anglo-Jewish relations? If this were true, it would be a nice example of the kind of irony which Hegel liked to discover in history. It would also go far to justify those wits who assert that a statue should be erected to Ernest Bevin as the real founder of the State of Israel—upside down, with his head in the sand. But his role was not as important—or as ugly—as that.

In assessing that role, it is important to remember one fact that Israelis naturally tend to forget. At any time during 1946 Ernest Bevin could have smashed

84

Jewish resistance and imposed British rule on Palestine for another ten or fifteen years. In June of that year, for example, the Haganah leaders—against the advice of Chaim Weizmann—decided to demonstrate the strength and efficiency of their forces by blowing up all the Jordan bridges in one night and thus isolating the British forces. The temptation to hit back was very strong and Mr. Bevin's military advisers assured him that the air force and tanks at their disposal were amply sufficient to smash every *kibbutz,* while the rest of the Army broke resistance in the cities. It is to the credit of Mr. Bevin that he refused to permit the orgy of destruction pressed on him by some of his military advisers. Unlike his successor in 1956, Mr. Bevin realised that Britain was no longer in a position to "go it alone" and impose her will in the Middle East by force of arms. So when he found he could not bully the Jews into acquiescence, he decided to cut his losses. The way in which the British withdrawal was organised was disgraceful. But at least when the Mandate was wound up and the last British soldier withdrew, Britain retained her paramountcy in the Middle East and there was still a chance, if the lesson of this dreadful episode had been learnt, to make a virtue of necessity and end British hegemony voluntarily, on the Indian model.

What Ernest Bevin ensured by his anti-Jewish vendetta was that the State of Israel should be compelled to fight a war of independence without the protection of a great power. Yet very soon it was clear that the unnatural and cruel conditions under which the new nation was brought to birth had two inestimable advantages. In the first place, the fact that the Jews of Palestine were compelled to fight and to win a war of independence proved to the Western world that they were indeed a nation. We have seen already that, particularly in Britain, it was widely held that the Jews who had settled in the National Home were a religious or, at best, an ethnic community and therefore not entitled to national self-determination. As far as I know, there is only one test of whether an ethnic community is indeed a nation. That test is war. The community must show that it is worthy of nationhood by fighting for its existence, even when the chances of survival are small. It was Ernest Bevin, the man who believed that it was only a religious community, who compelled the Yishuv to pass this test triumphantly. Moreover, the war of independence brought a second and equally important advantage to the new nation. It demonstrated that Israel was not, as her Arab neighbours believed, a British satellite, the advance guard of British imperialism in the Middle East. If the Jews of Palestine had achieved nationhood peacefully, under British protection, the new state would not have been able within ten years to break through the Arab blockade and establish relations with such kindred new nations as Burma and Ghana. There is nothing like a clash with Western imperialism to establish the credentials of a new member of the United Nations!

86

IX

One consequence of the war of independence for which Ernest Bevin can take full credit was the final transfer of leadership from Chaim Weizmann to David Ben-Gurion. The aspects of Weizmann's personality that so superbly matched the hour in 1917 disqualified him as a leader of his people against Ernest Bevin. The moment that the report of the Anglo-American Commission was rejected by the Labour Government, Weizmann's leadership was ended. For from that point on there was no possibility that the Jewish state would emerge under British protection. Leadership now passed to men who were versed in armed resistance.

It is widely believed that the main difference between Weizmann and Ben-Gurion was their attitude to Britain, with the former believing in the British connection and the latter anxious to break it. In my view, this interpretation falsifies the character of both men. The truth is that Ben-Gurion wanted co-operation with Britain as much as Weizmann. Where he differed was on the methods to be employed in achieving that co-operation. Weizmann, with his liking and respect for the British ruling class, found it difficult to believe that a British government could be blackmailed into concessions or forced to make them by resorting to violence. Ben-Gurion, who felt himself at home not with the British aristocracy but with the British labour move-

87

ment, had a much shrewder estimate of the factors determining British colonial and foreign policy. Moreover, as the politician chiefly responsible for organising the Haganah and fighting the Irgun, he did not share the repugnance that Weizmann always felt against the use of physical force.

No one who knew Weizmann could make the mistake of calling him a pacifist. In the Archives, I came upon a passage from the secret evidence he gave before the Peel Commission which I do not think has been previously published. It indicates how little he had in common with the sentimental pacifist. Here it is:

> If, in the interests of the British, the game is not worth the candle, then we can do nothing. Then we say we are sorry it does not pay you to do it. But we shall take the risk. We shall take our risk and every man, woman and child will fight for his existence here in Palestine. Nobody is stronger than the man who has got his back to the wall.

But although Weizmann could talk in this way—and mean it—as early as 1937, he knew that he was not the man to organise Jewish resistance. Indeed, he realised that the less he knew about the Haganah and the details of illegal immigration, the stronger would be his position in his negotiations with London. As we have now been reminded in Cyprus, it is not an unusual feature of resistance movements that the leader who negotiates with the oppressor government should be a man of peace, who deliberately and conscientiously averts his eyes from the deeds of violence done in his name.

Weizmann disliked not only the murderous terrorism of Begin's Irgun but the clean acts of violence undertaken by Ben-Gurion's Haganah. But the repugnance he expressed, both publicly and privately, was not that of the pacifist. I remember, for example, how he arrived in London just after the Irgun had blown up the British Headquarters in the King David Hotel, an exploit which claimed not only British and Arab but distinguished Jewish victims. Weizmann was staying, as usual, at his suite in the Dorchester Hotel, and two days after his arrival I went to see him. I found I was the first British politician to pay him a visit. Every one of his friends in the Conservative Party had discovered an excuse for absenting himself. So had those who claimed to be his friends among the members of the Labour Government. In his loneliness, he was touchingly pleased to see me, and when I mentioned the King David Hotel I suddenly saw that he was crying. As the tears streamed down his cheeks he said to me, "I can't help feeling proud of our boys. If only it had been a German Headquarters, they would have got the Victoria Cross."

This remark illuminates not only his attitude to the use of force but his complex feelings about Britain. It is amplified by a letter written a fortnight later, which has until now remained unpublished. The recipient was Chief Rabbi Herzog. Weizmann starts by thanking the Chief Rabbi for the account of his interviews with the Archbishop of Canterbury and Mr. Attlee. Then he goes on:

I have only just arrived in this country, and am not yet recovered from the shock of the last few weeks in Palestine, or from a hurried journey, so I hope you will forgive any gaps or other signs of haste in what follows.

Palestine today is not merely a police state: it is the worst form of military dictatorship. To all intents and purposes there is no Civil Administration; that has receded entirely into the background, and my impression is that the country is run by military cliques in Jerusalem and/or Cairo. . . .

When search was made on June 29th at Givat Brenner (a village only a few minutes by car from Rehovoth, so I can vouch for what happened there), the troops had been told they were to "occupy" it, and they behaved accordingly. They began to break into the schoolrooms and into a small laboratory which the children use; they broke into the girls' dormitory; pilfered watches, fountain-pens and other trinkets; tore or cut up clothing stored for the use of the *chalutzim,* and generally behaved like "conquerors." Characteristic of the whole proceedings here were the slogans used by the "invaders": "What we need is gas-chambers!" "Hitler didn't finish the job!" Swastikas were chalked or painted on walls (and also even on the pavements of Rehovoth—where I have seen them with my own eyes!). Everything was characteristic of troops preparing for "The Day."

It has been stated by the authorities that there was no intention in these searches of damaging the country's economy. It is difficult to believe this in view of the fact that in many settlements the whole male population has been carried away into detention, and is being kept in custody throughout the period of the harvest. It is my own view that, contrary to the official statements, the deliberate intention in these operations was to destroy as many of the settlements as possible. I believe that the recent operations were intended as the preliminary stage of something much larger. The military cliques expected a violent reaction to their first effort, a reaction such as would have justified the use of artillery, the bombing of Tel Aviv and other centres, and so on. But this was realised by the Yishuv, and although they were and are burning with indignation at the iniquities and indignities inflicted on them, they decided not to be "drawn," and maintained great restraint and rigorous discipline throughout. . . .

But I am afraid that since the events of Saturday, June 29th, the situation has changed fundamentally. Something has definitely snapped in the relationship between Jews and British in Palestine, and I, as a firm believer in, and champion of, that relationship, am forced to realise that what has been destroyed is so deep, so vital and of such moral significance, that it cannot be restored by projects, resolutions, and kind words.

I feel, therefore, that the only thing is to revert now to the Peel Report, which admitted that the British could not rule over the Jews, and that the only way to establish normal relations between the two peoples is to partition Palestine, and set up an independent Jewish State in treaty relations with Great Britain. What was true in 1937 is true, *a fortiori,* today, and it is the only way in which the situation may yet be saved. . . . Nothing else can clear the air now. What has happened in Palestine has been burnt into the soul of every man, woman and child in the Yishuv.*

From that letter we realise that what was broken and crushed by Ernest Bevin's policy was not the Israeli people but the personality of Chaim Weizmann. For whereas the Yishuv could survive the end of the British protectorate and be strengthened in the fire of the war, Weizmann's personality broke under the strain.

Yet his statesmanship was still to be essential in the winning of the war whose outbreak broke his heart. Those Israelis who criticise Weizmann as a mere diplomatist and claim that independence was achieved by force of arms should remember this. If Israel had not secured at the United Nations a majority decision in favour of partition and if the war of independence had not been fought in defence of this United Nations decision, Israel would not exist

* For full text see Appendix B.

today. Who achieved that majority vote at Lake Success? Not the terrorists of the Irgun or the soldiers of the Haganah but the aged leader of international Jewry, who could still shame and magic the Gentile world into recognizing its duty to his people. Here was the final contribution of Weizmann to his people's emancipation. For the last time "the Chief" was in command, and though the brunt of the work was borne by his devoted team, headed by Moshe Sharett and David Horowitz, it was his diplomatic strategy that they followed; and at more than one critical moment his personal intervention was decisive. It was an astonishing achievement for a man in his state of health. For surely it was an infinitely more difficult job to achieve a two-thirds majority at Lake Success in 1947 than it had been thirty years earlier to persuade Lloyd George, Balfour and Milner to make the Balfour Declaration. And the military importance of Weizmann's achievement was that when the war of independence came six months later, the Israelis, defending themselves against those who sought to reverse a decision of the United Nations, were able to win the sympathy of the world. Even in this century of totalitarianism, a just cause is still worth a good many divisions. It was Weizmann and his political team who provided the firm basis of international law on which Ben-Gurion and his Army could win their war of independence.

III

The First Decade

DAVID BEN-GURION

How DOES Ben-Gurion's Israel compare with the Jewish state of the Zionists' dreams? What have the inheritors of Weizmann done with their inheritance?

Some may say these are unfair questions. Israel, after all, has been faced since 1948 with problems that no Zionist prophet foresaw and has had to overcome dangers which Weizmann, even in his gloomiest moments, never predicted. I saw a good deal of him in 1947, when the crucial negotiations were taking place in the United Nations, as well as during the closing phases of the war of independence, when he was living at Rehovoth. The birth of the state should have been the splendid climax of his life's work, but in fact the years from 1947 to 1949 were years of tragedy, frustration and growing anxiety. Despite failing health, he accomplished his diplomatic tasks at the United Nations with his usual skill. But he could not get over the rupture with Britain and he was haunted by the fear that the democratic community which he had watched grow up under British protection would now be corrupted by terrorism. If that happened, the politics of the new nation, when it finally emerged, would be dominated not by the old Jewish ideals of freedom and peace but by the new totalitarian realities of force and fraud.

These fears were intensified when Weizmann observed with what malignant care the British government was staging its withdrawal from Palestine in ways calculated to foment Arab disorders and disrupt the transfer of authority from the British officials to the new Jewish state. It would have been possible to organise the British withdrawal in such a way as to assist the peaceful partition of the country along the demarcation line laid down by the United Nations. But this was not the design of Mr. Bevin and the British administrators, huddled behind the barbed wire in "Bevingrad." Their purpose was to assist the Arab effort to overrun the whole country and to impede the Jews' defence of the areas allotted to them. No wonder Weizmann feared that, as a result of Operation Chaos, the Yishuv, if it survived at all, would suffer the same fate as the Irish and emerge from its war of independence distracted by civil strife between rival terrorists.

None of these fears was realised. Instead, out of the dust of war there emerged, fully grown and fully armed, the Jewish state of which Weizmann had been the major prophet. Even more remarkable, this new State was not a military dictatorship but a complete and complex Western democracy, whose citizens were already enjoying all the essential civic and personal liberties while the war of independence was still being fought out. The ancient myth had become fact, but this time the goddess had sprung from the head not of Jupiter but of Janus.

I

Israel is the smallest of the Western democracies, but her creation was the greatest democratic achievement of postwar history. Since 1945 many peoples, inhabiting vast areas, have been lost to totalitarianism; others, who, on achieving independence, tried to make democracy work, have lapsed into military dictatorship. If one excludes countries where the issue is still in doubt, such as India and Ghana, this tiny patch of Middle Eastern territory is the one stable addition that Western democracy has gained since 1945. Despite every obstacle, the impossible has been achieved. The warrior Israel of David Ben-Gurion is a complete fulfillment of Chaim Weizmann's peaceful aspirations.

There are two aspects of this modern miracle to which I would call attention. As we saw in discussing his vision of the Jewish state, Weizmann had firmly opposed those theorists and planners among the Zionist politicians who wanted to work out in advance the political, social and economic structure of the nation they were trying to create in Palestine. He had assumed that the National Home would grow organically under British protection until one day the cocoon would break and the new nation emerge. Had he foreseen that the birth of Israel would occur in the first days of a murderous war and in the face of every kind of opposition from the British protector, Weizmann might not have dismissed so nonchalantly the demand for a blueprint and advance planning. Ben-Gurion and his colleagues had to take over and administer whatever institutions were to hand. As a result, the new State of Israel was composed of two sharply conflicting elements. On the one hand, great segments of the British Mandatory administration, as well as British official and legal procedures, got themselves incorporated into it. To these Anglo-Saxon institutions were added the "state within a state" which the Jewish Agency and the Histadrut had created, at first for co-operation but, in the last years, for resistance to the Mandatory government. There was no time to sort out good from bad, far less to reshape these organisations for their new purpose within an independent nation. Everything was taken over as it stood, and the new government's prime care was inevitably concentrated not on civil administration but on transforming a jungle of resistance, intelligence and terrorist organisations into a homogeneous army.

In the first months this disorderly take-over was inevitable. What was not inevitable was the refusal, as the war danger receded, to impose a neat new order on the jumble of old and new, of British and of Jewish institutions. I have always thought it both strange and characteristic of Anglo-Jewish relations that the Israeli police force, for example, should still retain the old blue uniforms of the hated Palestine police, simply because so many of these uniforms were found in store when the state was formed. In much the same way, the law reports of the British

House of Lords remained essential reading for Israeli lawyers. One can see the same process at work in the Israeli Army. It not only took over the British military camps but the exterior forms of British uniforms, drill and Army procedure.

Yet this brand-new Jewish nation was in no way Anglicised. When it accepted, as a temporary expedient, these British institutions and procedures, it transformed them into an Israeli way of life. Israeli soldiers may wear British uniforms, but they have abandoned altogether the class structure that divides the British officer from the British private. The form may be British, but the content is Israeli.

II

There is, however, one essential aspect of British democracy which I think we can claim that the Israelis borrowed wholesale. Normally when a small people achieves its freedom, the first and most consuming issue of politics centres round the constitution. But in the months between the decision of the United Nations in November, 1947, and the end of the Mandate in May, 1948, no one in Palestine had time to bother about the constitution of the new state. No one even bothered about its name, which had to be thought up at the last moment! Now, more than ten years later, the constitutional issue is still unresolved. I gather there are certain great pundits still busily working on the draft.* But Israel is the only democracy in the world, with the exception of Great Britain, that operates without a written constitution. The reason, of course, is that the Jews of the National Home had been living their democracy for years under the British Mandate. So they had learnt that the wise democrat never bothers to improve his political institutions until he has to. He is busy on other things which are more important, and when one institution becomes obsolete, he prefers not to remove it by a surgical operation but to leave it to wither into ceremonial ineffectiveness, like the British monarchy.

It is only a people with no experience of freedom and no feeling for democracy—like the Germans—who believe that you can write a perfect constitution and who are always busy tidying up administrative tag ends. The Israelis know that no constitution, however perfect, can preserve liberty unless the people practise freedom in their individual and community life. And, provided a people has achieved this pattern of free living, they can preserve it under a most imperfect constitution or even with no written constitution at all.

In adopting the British attitude to written constitutions, however, the Israelis have not abandoned the

---

* Since I wrote this, the electorate has given the Mapai, headed by Ben-Gurion, a most impressive victory at the polls and it has been announced that the new Cabinet will set to work on completing the constitution. Nevertheless, I beg leave to doubt whether the job will really be carried out!

Jewish form of democracy, which had developed for years inside the Zionist movement. The Knesset may pay some attention to the British parliamentary procedures enshrined in Erskine May,* but Israel's party politics are wholly un-British and derive from Central Europe. A multiplicity of parties is fostered by a system of proportional representation in which the elector votes for the party list rather than the man. As against the British two-party system, with its bias in favour of strong government and against coalition, the Israelis have retained the Zionist passion for multiparty manoeuvres and shifting coalitions.

In a country constantly threatened by attack from outside and economic crisis, this brand of Central European politics would have proved fatal had it not been for the stabilising influence of a British-style Labour Party, closely linked with the huge amalgamation of trade unions, co-operatives and industrial enterprises of the Histadrut. Here again the English visitor cannot resist a purr of satisfaction at the stubborn reluctance of the Israelis to modify the indefensible. That after a decade there should still be no system of free secondary education and that the Health Service should still be run by the Histadrut —all this must seem monstrous to a tidy-minded German Social Democrat or a Scandinavian trade

---

* I am proud to claim that the first clerk of the Knesset borrowed my copy of the new edition of Erskine May when it was out of print—and still has it!

unionist. Only the Englishman accepts it as homely and natural.

In recent years Ben-Gurion has let it be known that the trials to which multiparty politics subjects a Prime Minister have rendered him impatient. The Prime Minister, we are told, would like to introduce a system of single-member constituencies on the British model and would welcome a development away from the multiparty and towards the two-party system. This reform would certainly Anglicise Israeli politics, but at the cost of violating the respect for organic growth which has so far been a common tradition of British and Israeli democracy. In the deepest sense, nothing could be more un-British than to impose the British two-party system on the Jewish political life of Israel. Indeed, if this were done without simultaneously breaking up the power concentrated in the hands of the labour leaders who control the Mapai, the result would be to create the semblance without the reality of two-party government. For the essential principle of the British system is that there should be a *real* alternative Government, which has a *real* chance of expelling the party in office and achieving an outright majority. A permanent Government, faced by a permanent Opposition, is neither British nor democratic, but it might well be the result of an attempt to force Israeli party politics into the rigid framework of a British two-party system. The present party political system or lack of system is as higgledy-piggledy as Israel's unfinished constitution, but I believe it truly reflects the ethos of the Jewish community in Palestine and so provides the explanation of how the new state was able to survive, in the first months of its existence, the supreme test of war.

III

This brings me to the second aspect of this modern miracle to which I would call attention—the fact that terrorism ceased the moment independence was achieved. Here again, the experience of Israel is unique. Not only in Ireland but in almost every other small nation liberated by a resistance movement, the tradition of terrorism dies hard. Moreover, the Israeli resistance was not only highly organised and numerous, it permeated the whole life of the Yishuv. Thousands of young men and women had been trained to illegal violence and learnt to lie and to spy, to bribe the police and corrupt the established authorities. True, as we have seen, those in the Haganah, as distinct from the Irgun and the Stern Gang, had been trained to disapprove of terrorism and to regard themselves as members of a national army in the service of a national state. Yet it is remarkable that the moment the need for resistance and illegal activity was over, all these young men and women went back to their normal occupations and reverted to the normal standards of civic right and wrong. The fact that they were able to do so was the finest tribute to the organic Zionism which—

largely thanks to Weizmann's leadership—had become the philosophy of the National Home. Under the Mandate the Jewish community had taken root. In modern history it is only the rooted community, the people who have really become a nation, that can fight for its freedom and then return quietly to civil life. It is the unrooted and the volatile that bring back with them into their peacetime occupations the violence and corruption of war.

There is a phrase used by the Communists, "people's democracy." The only democracy I know which could literally and accurately be called a "people's democracy" is the State of Israel—at least during its first decade. The Western democracies are old nations which have grown up over many generations and which—even in the New World—have many aspects which are far from popular. Israel is a "people's democracy" because it is too young to have created an aristocracy, a ruling class or a social élite and too poor to be ruled by a plutocracy.

Of course, this makes Israel unstable, yet despite its instability, the new state is not less free than either Britain or America. The Israeli judiciary is certainly as independent as the American and almost as independent as the British. Press liberty, freedom of speech, freedom of thought, minority rights—all these sophisticated liberties are not talked about but taken for granted, in much the same way that we do in Britain. New nations and nations new to freedom are usually excited by the experience and talk about how thankful they are for what they have gained.

The Israelis are not even grateful for their liberties. They grumble all the time, thereby revealing how rooted their nation is in the idea of freedom. Moreover, they have added to our Western liberties a liberty which usually emerges only for a transition period in a postrevolutionary situation. The one kind of freedom which the Western democracies, with their stable social systems and exaggerated individualism, cannot enjoy is the sense of mass participation in the activities of the community. In the early days of the Chinese as well as of the Russian Revolution, this sense of mass participation was vivid and genuine. Since then it has been rapidly destroyed or perverted, as the Communist revolutions settled down into totalitarian regimes. Israel is the only country I know where this sense of mass participation has been combined with Western freedom and survived, at least for a decade, the revolutionary war during which the state was founded. The reason, of course, has been the Ingathering of the Exiles, the stream of new immigrants, which has more than doubled the population within ten years and has thereby prevented the nation from settling down into those social class distinctions and settled allocation of privileges which give the citizen of a Western democracy his individual freedom but at the same time alienate him from the community. As a result of this sense of mass participation, the young Israeli who comes to the West to study sometimes feels himself lonely. He resents the atomisation of social life which is one of the most dangerous characteristics of the American "affluent society" and of the more moderate material prosperity of postwar Britain.

IV

I have no doubt whatsoever that the institution which is mainly responsible for keeping this sense of mass participation alive is the Army. Here is one aspect of the new Israel which would have profoundly surprised Weizmann if he had lived to see it—and also made him deeply proud. As we saw in my second chapter, he was not a military man but, on the other hand, he had not a trace of the pacifist in him. He was an outsider when it came to discussing the technical details of war or resistance, and to this ignorance was added an acute anxiety lest the freedoms of the embryonic Jewish democracy should be destroyed by strong military leadership and lest terrorism should become an endemic disease. Personally, Weizmann was excluded from participating in the birth of Israel because the kind of leadership he could give was now required not in Palestine or in London but only at the United Nations. And to the disappointment which this engendered in him there was added a bitter anxiety lest the nation in whose birth the Army played the most important role should become militaristic.

I was among those of Weizmann's friends who remembered Ireland and shared his fears, particu-

larly when I saw that there was no prospect of end-
ing the state of war between Israel and her Arab
neighbours. Yet our fears have proved unjustified.
Although the Army has become by far the most influential single institution in the new state, not even the
bitterest opponents of Israel have accused its leaders
of militarism or suggested that there is any danger
of its representative institutions lapsing into military
dictatorship. I know of no other young nation whose
young men and women have been so obviously influ-
enced in their thinking, as well as in their bearing,
by their military training. The visitor has only to
give a few lifts to hitchhikers as he travels up and
down the country in order to realise that every Israeli
under forty is a trained soldier, most of them sea-
soned by more than one active campaign and all of
them ready for immediate recall at a few hours' notice. In Britain or North America, soldiering means
going overseas, and home defence is an unreal concept. In Israel it is the first, most urgent and most
continuous obligation of every citizen. The fiction
into which we escape when we watch a "Western"
film is everyday reality in a country where no one
lives more than twenty-five miles from a hostile
frontier.

That is why I add, as a third miracle in the history
of the first decade, the fact that in Israel there has
emerged a way of life that is military without becoming militaristic. Moreover, although the Army's
main function is home defence, it has developed a
second social purpose of almost equal importance.

III. *The First Decade*

Americans are fond of telling us that their country is a melting pot into which peoples of varying language and race are poured and out of which emerges a single, homogeneous nation. One has only to observe the Jews in New York, the Poles in Detroit or the Negroes in Atlanta to see that this claim is somewhat exaggerated. Integration of the immigrant is certainly a far speedier process in the United States than it is in Britain. But it is always a matter of generations, and even when the brew is complete, there remain some indigestible lumps in the porridge. The comparison with Israel is instructive. True, the process of integration in the Jewish state has been facilitated by the fact that all its immigrants were Jews. But, as the Israeli courts have recently discovered, it is by no means easy to find the common characteristic which differentiates the Jew from the non-Jew. That characteristic is certainly not religion (at least eighty per cent of the Israelis are agnostic). Nor can we detect either a common race or a common cultural tradition which unites the Westernised German or Polish Jews, many of them fair-haired, blue-eyed and round-headed, with their brothers from Morocco, Iraq or the Yemen. The Israelis, in fact, are bound together by one salient fact—that they were unwanted in the countries where they were born. And, from this point of view, the Ingathering of the Exiles into Israel bears a closer resemblance to the filling up of the United States than many Americans would like to admit. At the very least, it could hardly be denied that the unwanted hundreds of thousands who have poured into Israel since 1948 were as varied in their background as the unwanted millions who became American citizens before the quota laws closed the frontiers of the United States.

It is against this background that we can measure the achievement of the Israeli Army in licking this gallimaufry of newcomers into a citizen militia, normally scattered at its peacetime functions but capable, at a few hours' notice, of forming a striking force with the capacity of marching either to Baghdad or to Cairo. No nation can grow away from the traditions it acquires during the tumultuous years of its birth, and the Jewish state is no exception to this rule. Not only will its freedoms always be rooted in its citizen Army. The fabric of its social life and the quality of its civic virtues are those of a people for whom the bearing and the using of arms are not something abnormal but a natural part of everyday life. For the Israelis, peace is the abnormal interruption of a usual state of war, and the Army is the institution which indoctrinates the newcomer in the life of the frontier which is henceforth to be his normal existence.

What a different fate from that of the Jew who acquired an American passport and settled in New York and who only learns about the frontier in his history books or at the films! Once again I am struck by the irony of history. When Balfour and Weizmann envisaged the National Home, and even when Lord Peel recommended partition, it was always assumed that Palestine would be inhabited by Jews and Arabs living as intermingled communities and with the Arabs forming the majority of the population. How well I remember the occasion in 1946 when, in the presence of Ben-Gurion and Sharett, Weizmann showed me a map on which the partition line recommended by the Jewish Agency was sketched out. Of course it included the Negev, but on the first day of this Jewish state, as defined by Jewish leaders, the Arabs would be in a majority and Jewish immigration would have to proceed extremely rapidly in order to keep pace with the Arab birth rate. Inevitably such a state, if created under British protection—or, after 1948, under the United Nations—would have been binational, and very soon we should have seen the new, independent Arab-Jewish State of Palestine developing along the lines of its northern neighbour Lebanon, where rival racial and religious groups are held together in a balance of power guaranteed by the skilled manipulation of a complex constitution.

V

I must admit that in 1946, when I helped to draft the Report of the Anglo-American Commission, it was my aim to create a binational State of this kind. At that time, particularly on the Left, we were all much more internationalist than we are today—more hopeful about the United Nations and other international institutions, more conscious of the excesses of nationalism as we had seen them in Hitler's Germany. So, although I appreciated the strength of both Jewish and Arab nationalism, I convinced myself that it would be possible to create conditions for their co-existence by partitioning Palestine into one Arab and another Jewish-Arab State. It still seems to me that this was the solution which the Labour Government should have attempted. But I am less sure now than I was then that the attempt would have been successful. The Arabs in the purely Arab part of the country might well have been happy to have become part—as they actually have done—of an enlarged Hashemite Kingdom of Jordan. But would the Arabs of the new binational State have stood by and permitted the Jews to introduce half a million new immigrants and thereby achieve an absolute majority? Perhaps by adopting this solution all Ernest Bevin would have achieved would have been to postpone the Arab-Jewish war and the creation of a Jewish State burdened with a hostile Arab minority.

As things turned out, however, the Israeli can with perfect fairness insist that the reduction of the Arab population of Israel to this inferior status was the result not of anything they willed or did but solely of Ernest Bevin's policy. Even after he had transferred the Palestine problem to the United Nations and the UNSCOP majority report had been voted in the Assembly by the necessary two-thirds majority, the British Foreign Secretary refused to accept defeat. Instead of helping to divide the country along the frontiers laid down by the United Nations, the British soldiers and administrators in Palestine were encouraged from London to make the UN decision inoperative. It was with their connivance that hundreds of thousands of Arabs were instructed by their leaders to become temporary refugees, while the Arab armies drove the Jews into the sea. But those "temporary refugees" have never been able to return to their homes and most of them still sit idly in the UNRWA camps today. Instead of the new Jewish State starting, as UNSCOP intended that it should, with rather more Arab than Jewish inhabitants, Israel is now left with only an insignificant Arab minority, concentrated for the most part in the mountains of Galilee.

What part do these Arabs of Israel play in Israeli democracy? Economically they have prospered; and sharing, as they do, in the Jewish welfare state, they enjoy a far higher standard of living than their fellow countrymen in any Arab State. Nor can they complain about any deprivation of political or civil rights. All of them—including the women—vote in national and local elections, and Arabic is a recognised second language in the Israeli Knesset. In addition to full religious freedom, they also enjoy the right to produce their own Arabic newspapers and have their own Arab social institutions. Officially, the only important discrimination employed against them is the severe control and limitation of their movements, on which the Israeli Army still insists.

Nevertheless, it would be silly to pretend that the Arabs of Israel feel themselves equal citizens of this national Jewish State. On the contrary, if the Syrians or Jordanians marched into Galilee, they would be received as liberators by virtually the whole Arab population, despite the fact that liberation would involve a sharp lowering of the standard of life. Ten years after the war ended, these Arab villagers are still a "fifth column" inside Israel, and one cannot be surprised that the Army and police insist on treating them as such. Nor can one hope that the lapse of time will soften their sense that they are the unwilling subjects of a conquering Jewish race. How could they think otherwise, when, in order to achieve higher education or social advancement, they must not only learn Hebrew but betray their national heritage by accepting the Jewish way of life? To grow up an Arab, an ambitious boy must remain a villager in Israel or escape across the frontier to Beirut or Cairo University.

In the first years after the birth of the Jewish State, I was sharply critical of Ben-Gurion's attitude to the Arab minority and shared the view of the Left-Wing Socialists of Mapam that this blot on Israeli democracy could be removed by a policy of patient, systematic conciliation. "If you put your democracy and your socialism into practice in your treatment of the Arabs," I said, "they are bound to respond." I now realise that, in giving this advice, I was grossly underestimating the strength of Arab nationalism and the depth of the hatred and revulsion aroused in the Arab mind by the Jewish victory. The truth is that, once most of the Arab population had fled and Jewish immigrants had taken their place, Israel was bound to develop as a state in which an Arab, even if he achieved complete social and economic equality, would still feel himself a second-class citizen and still behave as a potential enemy.

It is this that explains the obvious but superficially baffling relief with which Ben-Gurion withdrew his troops from the Gaza strip after the Suez campaign. I happened to be visiting Israel at the time and spent a long day seeing how the Arabs in Gaza and around the town were adapting themselves to Israeli occupation. On my return to Tel Aviv I discussed the problem with several members of the Cabinet. Would it not be possible, I suggested, that the Gaza strip should be integrated into Israel on condition that its Arab population were offered the free choice between becoming full citizens of Israel or being moved by UNRWA to an Arab State of their choosing? Of course it is dubious whether this plan would have been acceptable to the Arabs. But what interested and surprised me at the time was the unanimity with which the Israeli turned it down. So far from regarding the Gaza strip and its Arab population as spoils of war, which should if possible be retained in peace, they talked of them as dangerous hazards, to be returned to the United Nations as soon as possible. I was puzzled until I was told that the addition of nearly 200,000 souls to the Arab minority would not only increase its absolute strength but quite possibly make it the balancing factor in Israel's complex multiparty political system. Israel, I was forced to

116

realise, had become a self-consciously Jewish state and, rather than increase its Arab population, any Israeli Government will deny itself extensions of territory. Ironically enough, the exclusiveness of Israeli nationalism is the best guarantee the Arabs possess against the threat that Israel will ever launch an expansionist war.

Once again we observe how many of the main characteristics of this new State have been imposed upon it by duress. It was only because the Jews of Palestine were compelled to create the State of Israel in the face of the Arab Armies that this state acquired its exclusively Jewish national character. It was only because, in the throes of war, most of the Arab population fled that room was made for the million and more immigrants whose presence has made the remaining Arabs an insignificant minority. Finally, it was only because continued Arab belligerency made the Army the central institution of Israel that an instrument was fashioned powerful enough to mould the disparate elements of the new immigration into a united nation. In my second chapter I suggested that those who call Ernest Bevin the unwitting founder of Israel were giving him undue importance. But it is no exaggeration to say that the integration of the new immigrants into a free nation, militarised yet not militaristic, can be attributed largely to Arab hostility. Without that curtain of hatred which surrounds Israel and forces on its citizens their tough frontier mentality, the new state might have taken on the urban and commercial characteristics of its immigrants and become an easygoing Levantine community such as the Arab world could easily assimilate. Once again necessity has been the mother of invention and the Yishuv was compelled, if it was to survive at all, to become a nation not of individualistic shopkeepers and peasants but of Socialist settlers, trained to war.

VI

I fancy one can trace the working of that same historical irony in the economic history of Israel's first decade. Once again, in order to measure the real achievement, it may be useful to compare what has actually happened with the expectations of the Zionists before 1948. In Weizmann's conception, for example, there were three conditions for the economic success of the National Home. First, the Jews of Palestine must have free access to the markets of the Middle East. Secondly, they must not be burdened with a heavy military budget but be able to rely on British protection until peaceful relations with the Arabs had been achieved. Thirdly, there should be a steady but not too heavy flow of immigration.

Not one of Weizmann's three conditions has been fulfilled in the last ten years. All Israel's natural markets, where she could buy the foodstuffs she lacked and where her industries could compete on favourable terms, have been cut off by the Arab cold war. The government has been compelled to raise the military budget until the proportion of the national resources devoted to defence is one of the highest in the world. Finally, immigration has been of a dimension which no one even dared to conceive as a practical possibility before 1948.*

Despite these adverse circumstances, the economic position has improved out of all recognition, and nowhere is this clearer than in agriculture. In 1948, for example, Israel was producing just under fifty per cent of its food requirements. By 1959 the figure

* I cannot resist giving one example of the kind of prognosis then current even among those who were sympathetic to Zionism: "The success of the National Home has been partly due to the selection and training of the immigrants. To turn it into a 'dumping ground' for unwanted Jews would destroy its unique qualities. I believe, therefore, that the bulk of the Jews who wish to leave Europe, like the homeless Poles and Balts and Jugoslavs, should go west to the New World, like their fathers before them, and that, after the first 100,000 enter Palestine, an independent Jewish Commonwealth, if established, would be bound to return to a policy of highly selective immigration. The greatest help which Britain and America can give to Palestinian Jewry would be to tackle the refugee problem, and so relieve Palestine of an impossible burden." This passage comes from my own book, *Palestine Mission*, which I wrote in the summer of 1946. Seldom has a prediction been more thoroughly falsified by history. But in fairness to myself, I recall that the view which I put on paper was very widely held. Even when the state was founded in 1948, few—outside the Arab propagandists—took Ben-Gurion seriously when he talked about an ingathering of a million exiles. Yet the actual figure by the end of the first decade was 922,274.

had improved to seventy per cent, though meanwhile the population had trebled! Indeed, I am informed that the government is now gravely disturbed by the excess production of milk and eggs. No doubt agricultural surpluses of this kind present a problem—but it is a much more agreeable problem than those which Israel faced ten years ago!

How have these surpluses been achieved? After many years of unsuccessful imports and experiments in crossbreeding, a Frisian cow has been evolved which can stand the climate and whose average annual milk yield is rather better than that of the British Frisian herds. But even today the cost to the community of these successes has not been small. Israeli production of broilers and of eggs, as well as of milk, is still far too dependent on imported feeding stuffs acquired cheap, thanks to American aid. It is characteristic of this impatient little country that already there are voices calling for a completely new agricultural policy, which would break away from mixed farming and concentrate on industrial crops, such as cotton and groundnuts. If these demands are even partially met, it will involve even greater political and social adjustments than we have so far seen. Already since 1948, the role of the completely collectivised *kibbutz* in agricultural development has declined and that of the *moshav,* or co-operative village, correspondingly increased. A movement towards industrial crops will surely bring with it an increased role for the great state or private company managing large units of land.

What effect will all this have on the fabric of Israeli society? As we have seen, its institutions were evolved to meet a series of emergencies: the purpose of the *kibbutz,* for example, was threefold—to provide an organisation in which urban Jewish intellectuals could become land workers, to develop completely "unprofitable" land, and to establish settlements of strategic importance. The simplicity—often poverty—of *kibbutz* life was willed only by a minority of the members. The vast majority accepted the hardships as inseparable from pioneering. It is natural enough, therefore, that the organisation of agriculture should be radically transformed as Israel moves from pioneering into a more stable stage of development. And here I have noticed another trait which has been borrowed from England. Like us, the Israelis make their big changes while they assert the opposite. The *Kibbutz,* we are told, will always remain a central feature of Israeli life. In this way the traditionalists are given some satisfaction, even while their status is being undermined.

VII

Yet, despite these achievements, the expert view is that without a miraculous increase in the water supply—by desalinisation, for example—the top limit of agricultural settlement has been nearly reached. Output per acre and per man will, no doubt, be further improved, but this will be done without greatly increasing the proportion of the population who get their living from the land. If this expert prediction is correct, one conclusion follows. Since more and more of the new immigrants must in future be placed in industry, the future of Israel depends on a new industrial revolution. This must establish modern industries which do not require expensive imported raw materials and whose quality and price make it possible for them to compete not in the backward markets of the Middle East but in the West, where competition is more severe.

In normal circumstances industrialisation of this kind would be out of the question. But when I observe how Israel responded to the challenge of the first decade, I see no reason why the same kind of thing should not happen in the second. Nor should anyone imagine that this is something to do with Jewish peculiarities. The truth is that a vital nation whose survival is threatened nearly always responds "miraculously" to the challenge. The only European state created under almost as unfavourable circumstances as Israel is Western Germany. And which of us has not heard of the *Wirtschaftswunder?* Like Palestine, Germany was partitioned and millions of its inhabitants turned into homeless, destitute refugees. It is instructive to compare the German and the Arab reactions to these disasters. Fatalistically, the Arab states accepted the influx of refugees and then left them in the care of UNRWA, confining their energies to a political demand for the restoration of all they had lost in the war. How differently the

West Germans reacted to a much more annihilating defeat and an even larger influx of destitute refugees into their partitioned country! Their upward climb has been as rapid as that of Israel. It is natural enough for a democracy, in which the trade-union movement is powerful, to cut immigration down to a trickle in order to maintain working-class living standards. But the effect of closing the door is soporific—where there is no challenge there is no corresponding response and no economic miracle. Those who are surprised by the recent signs of *rapprochement* between the Israelis and the Western Germans should not forget the affinity of experience in the first decade of their existence, which unites Israel and the Federal Republic and which has created a bond between the Jews and their onetime exterminators.

We must assume, therefore, that the "crazy" policy of unlimited immigration into Israel will continue—even if it involves, as it conceivably might, the acceptance one day of a million Jews from Russia. Will this lead, as the Arabs fear, to a chauvinist demand for extended frontiers? One reason for giving a negative answer has been stated already.* Another is the obvious fact that the inclusion even of large arid areas of adjacent Syrian and Jordanian territory would do little towards any permanent solution of Israel's population problem. As the Jews themselves have found to their own cost, agricultural

* See page 117.

settlement of urban immigrants is as expensive as it is slow, and the proportion of Israelis who are suited to a rural life seems no greater than that in any Western country. What is needed, therefore, is not more territory but more industrial activity. And in Israel, with its dearth of natural resources, this can be achieved only by reliance on brain power, science and technology.

In my first chapter, we saw that Weizmann's scientific activities were not separate from his Zionism but an essential part of it. A small Jewish state, with its unique immigration laws, could only prosper, he foresaw, if its indigenous science and technology were equal in quality to those of the biggest and wealthiest Western powers. Hence his determination to maintain standards in the Institute he founded at Rehovoth which many of his friends regarded as quite unrealistic for a tiny people in a notch of the Middle East. Hence too his determination to ensure that the Hebrew University did not degenerate into a theological seminary.

Today, after the first decade, Weizmann's inheritors can proudly claim that they have fulfilled the terms of his testament. In the Haifa Technion, the Hebrew University, the Weizmann Institute, Israel possesses three institutions of higher education and research which set a standard for all the under-developed peoples of Asia and Africa and which prove triumphantly that the secret places of modern science need not remain a monopoly of the great powers. It is no accident that Israeli architects and craftsmen have been permitted to lavish on the buildings in which these institutions are housed money and skill which would have been attacked as absurd extravagance if they had been spent on any other activity. The government has recognised that the industrial revolution which Israel now needs cannot be accomplished by borrowing new technologies from abroad but will depend on the creation of an indigenous élite of scientists, technologists and engineers. Jewish Israel is the one democracy whose very existence requires that its policies should be shaped by an aristocracy of intellect.

VIII

I now turn from the achievements of the first decade to its failures. There is no doubt what has been the greatest disappointment in these last ten years—Chaim Weizmann would have called it a tragic disappointment. One of the central themes of his Zionist philosophy was that the National Home was not only a Jewish need—it was essential also to the renaissance of the Arab world. It was his notion that Israel should become the pilot plant in which should take place experiments in agriculture, in the reconquest of the desert, in the industrialisation of a backward area and in collective living required to revive the vanished glories of Middle Eastern civilisation. Not one tittle of this vision has come true. On the contrary, instead of collective competition be-

tween Jew and Arab, we have seen the development
of a sterile racial war in which Arab anti-Zionism
has been slowly degenerating into something re-
markably similar to Christian anti-Semitism.

In the first years after the birth of the state, it was
possible to feed on the illusion that, despite the
frontier of hatred that had split Palestine, Israel was
a "sociological time bomb" whose historical function
was to detonate the long-delayed Arab social revolution. True enough, we have seen since 1948 anti-
Western military *coups d'état* first in Cairo and then
in Baghdad. The Nasser-Neguib *Putsch* was directly
motivated by the disgraceful defeat of the Egyptian
Army in Palestine, and Brigadier Kassem's success
was made a great deal easier by the belief that Nuri
Said's masters in London were guilty of collusion
with Israel during the Suez venture. Nevertheless,
it is difficult any longer to pretend that either
the existence of Israel or the defeat of the corrupt
cliques which dominated the Arab world in 1948
has strengthened the tiny number of progressive
Arabs who believe in a democratic social revolution.
Alas, the constructive response to the challenge of
1948 has been entirely on the Jewish side of the
frontier. On the Arab side, half a million refugees
feed their hatred on nostalgic hopes of revenge. We
have seen how, by refusing to impose partition and
create a Jewish state under imperial protection,
Ernest Bevin became an unwitting and unwilling
co-founder of Israel—enlarging its frontiers, reduc-
ing the Arab population to a small minority and

steeling the young democracy in the fires of a fear-some war. In terms of internal and domestic develop-ments, the results of the war of independence—and of its logical consequence, the Sinai campaign—have been mostly beneficial. But externally the new nation has had to pay a dreadful price for the victories over the Arab Armies which Mr. Bevin and then Sir Anthony Eden foisted on it.

This price has been increased by the pressure of world events on the Arab-Jewish conflict. It is the fact that the local cold war between Arab and Jew has become part of the world cold war which has made the problem utterly insoluble and driven Israel to accept once again protection from the West. In the first months of the state's existence, a foreign policy of non-identification was proclaimed. In those early days, Israel's new government was able to say, "We don't want to huddle under anybody's protec-tion now that we have won our war of independ-ence. We have now disproved the Arab charge that we are stooges of British imperialism. By standing up to oppression and kicking the British out, we have also earned the genuine friendship of Britain, as the Irish and the Boers earned it before us. Our toughness, moreover, has won us the recognition both of the United States and of the Soviet Union. We intend, if possible, to obtain the confidence of East and West and thereby to fulfill our main func-tion of providing a homeland to which the rich Jews of the Western world can contribute their dollars (and, if possible, a few of their children) and the poor Jews of the Eastern bloc can come in person."

"Non-identification," in fact, developed organically and inevitably out of the conditions in which Israel achieved her independence. But this policy was whittled away by the intensification of the cold war. In 1950 the North Korean aggression forced Ben-Gurion to choose between loyalty to the charter of the United Nations and the principles of Western democracy, on the one hand, and perseverance in non-identification, on the other. He chose the former and Israel began to rely more and more on Western protection. Simultaneously the Soviet Union abandoned its reliance on a Communist-organised social revolution in the Arab world and began systematically to exploit Arab xenophobia and Arab anti-Zionism as instruments for expelling Britain from the Middle East.

I am inclined to believe that before King Abdullah was murdered there was a real chance of a separate peace between Israel and Jordan. With considerably more hesitation I accept the view that in the early months of the Egyptian revolution General Neguib did not exclude the possibility of serious negotiations with Ben-Gurion. But even if these early chances of peacemaking were not illusory, they had disappeared by the end of 1953. With America and Russia on the edge of war, there was no prospect whatsoever that Arab and Jew, even if they wanted to, could be brought to a rational agreement. The legacy of Mr. Bevin's policies was, at least in some respects, beneficial. The legacy of Mr. Dulles's brinkmanship brought no advantage of any kind to Israel—unless we count it an advantage that the Arab world has thrown off first British and then, since 1956, American suzerainty. The greatest immediate benefit which Western policy could confer on Israel would be a relaxation of East-West tension and the settlement of one concrete problem (for instance, Berlin) in such a way as to prove that the coexistence of irreconcilables is a practical policy. Such an achievement would have immediate and direct repercussions on Arab-Jewish relations. But until the great powers play their part, there is very little which any Jewish statesman can do.

IX

Nevertheless, it is still useful to discuss whether Israel's abandonment of non-identification was a temporary concession to the cold war or involved a permanent change of policy. Has Israel grown, in this first decade of its life, into a "normal" Western democracy? Should it be the aim of Israeli statesmanship to overcome the obstacles which at present prevent her membership of NATO and even of the Common Market? Or does wisdom point in quite a different direction? Should the slackening in the cold war, which both America and Russia now seem to desire, be regarded as an opportunity for getting out from underneath the Western military umbrella and resuming a policy of non-identification?

Influential voices, outside as well as inside Israel, speak for the first alternative. Two rather different kinds of argument are employed. In the first place, we are told, it is essential to form the strongest possible military links either with NATO as a whole or with any individual great power that is willing to assist Israel. This strategic argument is sometimes supplemented by the warning that an Israel which sought to establish an independent position between the blocs and return to a policy of non-identification might well lose the confidence of American Jewry, on whose voluntary contributions its development so largely depends, as well as forfeit economic aid from the American administration.

For the moment I postpone consideration of these cogent arguments from expediency in order to deal with the ideological case for Western integration. This is less frequently and less loudly voiced in public, but in Israel its influence, especially on the younger generation, is extremely strong. We are reminded that, after a decade, we are no longer dealing with a National Home for unwanted Jews but with an Israeli nation, which is now firmly established as the only genuine Western democracy in the Middle East. Naturally the Israelis are not forgetful of their history or ungrateful for the support of the Diaspora. But they cannot permit world Jewry, through the Zionist organisations, to challenge their sovereignty. And their resistance to outside interference is all the stronger when they observe that few of the Western Jews who control and finance the Zionist organisations show any inclination either to work in Israel themselves or to encourage their children to become immigrants. Israel, the argument proceeds, does not challenge the right of Western Jewry to prefer the fleshpots. What it insists on is its own right to develop as a normal democracy and, if the national Israeli interest requires it, to integrate its military and economic life with the NATO powers. If non-identification can be proved a sound policy in terms of Israeli national interests, well and good. Otherwise it is unacceptable.

X

The presentation of these two alternatives makes one thing clear. It is impossible to discuss Israel's external relations so long as we skirt the ticklish issue of her relations with the Diaspora. What has the first decade brought forth to confirm or to refute the assumptions on which the National Home was founded? Has anti-Semitism, as the Zionists predicted, been sapped by the creation of a Jewish nation, living in a Jewish state? If one looks exclusively at the position of Western Jewry, these questions are not difficult to answer. The warnings of those wealthy Jews who opposed the Balfour Declaration, on the ground that it would undermine their status and security as British citizens, have not been fulfilled. As Weizmann predicted, the standing, the

self-confidence and the morale of Western Jewry
have been vastly strengthened by the existence of
Israel. Even more important, the stereotype of the
Jew as a clever cosmopolitan and slick money spin-
ner has been weakened in the Gentile mind by the
earthiness and toughness of Israeli democracy. The
victories of the Israeli Army have done more to combat anti-Semitism in Christian countries than the
combined effort of all the societies for reconciling
Christians and Jews put together. Thousands of Englishmen, for example, who regarded the Suez venture as a reckless crime could not suppress a glow of
admiration for the Sinai campaign.

The existence of a Jewish state has, in fact, had
precisely the effect in the Western world that Herzl
predicted. Nor is there any sign that the financial
contributions of Western Jewry, on which the rapid
development of Israel depends, will fade away. Just
because ninety-nine per cent of the Western Jews
feel safely rooted in their countries of adoption, they
are all the more inclined to salve their consciences
by heavy financial contributions to Zionist causes. In
terms of better relations with their Gentile neighbours, even those who have failed to give active support to Zionism have done very well out of the creation of Israel, and the sense of obligation this creates
is unlikely to diminish. After all, it is not often that
history permits a people to have its cake and to
eat it!

It is not surprising, however, that this should have
created some difficulties in Israel, particularly among

the younger generation. When I was in Jerusalem four years ago, I made a special point of discussing the Diaspora with a number of sabras. Nearly all of them expressed to me frankly and violently their contempt for the rich, comfortable Jews of the West and justified it by comic stories about Jewish visitors to Israel. One young man went so far as to say to me, "Really we are not Jews any more. We are Israelis." A Gentile who hears this sentiment expressed in Jewish Jerusalem feels a sense first of shock and then of slightly indecent gratification. For all of us, if we accept Chaim Weizmann's theory,* are latent anti-Semites. I, at least, could not avoid an inward smirk, and I could not help reminding this young Israeli that the description he had just given me of Western Jewry tallied point by point with Fascist propaganda. Unconsciously, he was revealing an inverted anti-Semitism, as distasteful as that of the assimilationist. For if it is a shameful thing for a Jew, ashamed of his Jewishness, to seek escape by becoming a Gentile, why is it any better to choose a "non-Jewish" Israel as the escape route?

Returning four years later, I was glad to find that these heretics (I am told the right name for them is Canaanites) had almost disappeared. The sabra, although he often displays a tough, uncomplicated anti-intellectualism, still retains his Jewishness, in particular his sobriety and proneness to dialectics. Nevertheless, it is still true that the young Israelis

* See page 14.

often feel more at home with Gentile visitors than they do with British or American Zionists. One day I was talking enthusiastically about the work of integration I had seen that morning in a village school. An expression of nausea spread across the face of the sabra in the café beside me. "So even Crossman talks Zionism," he observed, and then explained to me with charm and good humour that the worst thing anyone can be accused of, by his standards, was "talking Zionism." "Give me an example," I said, and he replied promptly, "The American Jew stops his car in a village, turns to his wife and says, 'Look, a Jew milking a cow! How wonderful!' What on earth does he think one does with a cow?" he concluded savagely. "That is what I mean by 'talking Zionism.'"

It is silly to blame the sabra for his impatience with the Western Jew, who inevitably retains many of those characteristics which the Zionists disliked as much as the Gentiles and of which the Israelis are free. But this impatience is not new or limited to the younger generation. As we saw in my first chapter, Weizmann himself found it difficult to suppress his dislike for the assimilated Western Jew, and reserved his affection for the minority who devoted themselves wholeheartedly to Zionism. Here is yet another characteristic which he shared with Ben-Gurion.* How, then, can those born in Israel be

* I cannot resist recalling what Ben-Gurion said to me when I visited him at his home in Tel Aviv on the last day before the Anglo-American Commission left Palestine for

expected to show more comprehension than their seniors?

If this lack of understanding, however, were permitted to degenerate into what I have described as "inverted anti-Semitism," it would endanger the relationship between Israel and the Diaspora, on which the whole future of the country depends. It is a wonderful thing that the Jew who lives in Israel should be rid of his inferiority complex and sense of second-class citizenship, but he cannot, without denying the essence of his nationhood, regard himself merely as an ex-Jew, or "Israeli Goy." The Israeli must be Jewish as well as Israeli, just as much as the American Jew must be Jewish as well as American. Those Zionists who believed that the creation of a Jewish state would cure the world of anti-Semitism and remove the frontier between Jew and Gentile were guilty of intellectual oversimplification. There are only two methods of eradicating anti-Semitism—either to exterminate the Jewish people or to assimilate them completely into the Gentile world. What the creation of Israel has done is to transform what was once an insoluble problem—good relations between Jew and Gentile—into a soluble problem. But the price of this tremendous achievement has

---

Lausanne. I was already in the car when he pushed his head over the window, grinned at me and said, "One last word. Remember we are not the Jews of the Bronx or Whitechapel. We are the ones who refused to live there. And if you want to get us right, imagine yourself out here, fighting for your national existence, and calculate that we shall behave as you would behave if you were in our situation."

been the creation of a new problem, the ever growing difference between the Jews of Israel and the Jews of the Diaspora.

It was also an illusion for the Zionists to believe that the Jew in his homeland would become a "normal" citizen of a democracy. This first decade has already shown quite clearly that the Israeli, no less than the Jew of the Diaspora, is a "peculiar" person, with an internal conflict to resolve of which no Gentile has any experience. To be a good Israeli, he must be a patriot, rooted in his homeland, and in this respect much closer to the Gentile than to the Jew outside. But simultaneously he must retain his Jewishness, his loyalty to the Diaspora and the sophisticated sense of nationhood which for hundreds of years preserved Jewry in exile. To be a good Israeli, in fact, is just as complex a problem as to be a good American or British Jew.

"Then why bother?" it may be asked. "People didn't come to Israel merely in order to grapple with the complex problem of Jewishness in a different climate. They came here to be rid of the problem." There is no reply to this argument, except to point out that an Israel which ceased to be Jewish would not merely be cut off from the financial aid on which rapid development depends. Provided that the state simultaneously stopped all further immigration, a denial of further economic assistance would not in itself be a bad thing. Much more important than the economic consequences is the fact that without the spur of its Jewishness the State of Israel, after a generation, would become another Levantine community, of no more significance than Lebanon.

I appreciate that these few remarks about Israel's Jewishness and her relations with the Diaspora will be dismissed as glimpses of the obvious by those Jews who do not resent them. In marked contrast with the sabras, the elder generation of responsible Jewish leaders, both in Israel and outside, is so reluctant to discuss this topic that they take offence even when Mr. Ben-Gurion alludes to it. Nevertheless, it is plainly impossible to reach any conclusions about Israel's external policy unless the central issue of her relations with the Diaspora is squarely faced. If Israel were merely a small Western democracy recently established in the Middle East, there could be no conceivable objection to a policy of military and economic integration with Western Europe. But if Israel is essentially a Jewish homeland, tied as closely to the Jews of the Soviet Union as it is to Western Jewry, then this question of membership of NATO and of the Common Market takes on a very different aspect. True enough, there is no prospect at the moment either of any direct negotiations with the Arabs or of an American-Russian *détente,* which could lay the foundations for a Middle Eastern peace settlement. But if Israel is still regarded as the Jewish homeland, at the very least no policy should be undertaken which would make a return to the policy of non-identification more difficult.

XI

Was the Sinai campaign a policy of this kind? I do not think so. As a method of pacifying the frontier, it did a power of good. What did harm was the appearance of collusion by Israel in an Anglo-French attempt to restore an imperial suzerainty over the Arabs that was utterly out of date. Ironically enough, the policies of both Sir Anthony Eden and Mr. Ben-Gurion were damaged by this appearance of underhand collaboration, and this is one reason why I doubt whether the collusion between these two statesmen went very far. The last thing Sir Anthony could have wanted to do was to undermine the position of his loyal ally, Nuri Said, by appearing to be working with the Israelis. Yet this is what he did by launching an attack on Egypt which showed foreknowledge of Israel's plans. It is equally difficult to see what Mr. Ben-Gurion gained by the arrival of that lumbering Anglo-French expeditionary force at Port Said. Certainly he required French air cover for Tel Aviv in order to undertake his punitive campaign in Sinai; and I have no doubt that there was Franco-Israeli cooperation at all levels. But the actions of Sir Anthony did Israel grave harm.

Yet some good has resulted from the shipwreck of British policy. The Suez venture marked the final end of British political and military paramountcy in the Middle East and thereby, for the first time since 1929, created the possibility for a genuinely friendly relationship between Britain and Israel. So long as Britain had Arab allies to assist or puppet states to protect, the temptation to appease them by concessions to anti-Zionism was irresistible. Harold Macmillan and David Ben-Gurion can now become firm friends because, so far as I know, we have no Arab allies left to whom we can profitably sacrifice Israeli interests.

Moreover, the end of British paramountcy in the Middle East has had none of the disastrous consequences, either to Britain or to Israel, which were so frequently predicted. For ten years I was a voice in the wilderness, preaching that we should withdraw from the Middle East as totally and completely as we had withdrawn from the Indian subcontinent. I said, of course, that such a withdrawal would involve the risk of Arab convulsions, which would provide the opportunity for Russian intervention. But I thought this was still a lesser evil and that, as we should be forced out anyway, the sensible thing was to win some credit by conceding voluntarily what would anyway be extracted from us. Up till the Suez venture, there was still a chance of the kind of voluntary withdrawal in the Middle East which is now being carried out in Africa. But after the withdrawal from Port Said and the murder of Nuri Said, we had no choice. Our ships pass through the Suez Canal by Colonel Nasser's permission. The oil flows from Iraq and Kuwait because the Arab rulers need the money it earns.

For years successive British Governments have felt

they had a civilising mission to improve the Arabs
and teach them the ways of democracy. Now they
have shown they want nothing to do with it, and it is
time that we learnt to apply what President Roosevelt
described as a Good Neighbour policy when he
adopted it towards Mexico and Latin America. The
Latin-American states, he told the State Department,
should be left free—free to be corrupt, to suffer under
dictatorships, to develop democracies, provided only
they did not constitute a threat to their northern
neighbour. Whether we like it or not, the Arabs,
since the Suez venture, have achieved the same kind
of independence. Fortunately for us, the strategic
importance of the Middle East to Britain has been
greatly reduced by Indian independence, and as for
oil, the Arabs need to sell it at least as much as we
need to buy it.

XII

What does all this mean to Israel's future? Certainly the dream that the function of the Jewish
state was to stand guard at a vital point of Britain's
imperial lifeline has lost any meaning it ever had,
and with it has disappeared the justification for
the hope that a Jewish state might one day be an
independent member of the Commonwealth. These
visions, which inspired Weizmann, at least in his
middle period, were never wholly repudiated by
Ben-Gurion so long as British power was a reality.

The difference between the two men was that Ben-Gurion was quicker to recognise the imminent end of Britain's Middle Eastern paramountcy and also foresaw that when Britain withdrew, the United States would not be able to fill the gap for long. Those who believe that it is Israel's function to be a military outpost of the West are logical enough when they turn their attention from Britain and the United States to France. For it is only the French who are still seeking to maintain an imperial relationship with the Arab world and who therefore could make use of Israel's military strength. No one, however, sees more clearly than Ben-Gurion the danger of a close alliance with France, which would link the destiny of Israel irrevocably and tragically with that of the European in French North Africa.

There is, however, one argument for military integration with the West which I have heard expounded by highly responsible Israelis. The decision to seek membership of NATO and a still closer military understanding with France, I have been told, is necessitated by the Russian determination to back Arab nationalism. The political advantages of a return to non-identification are not denied, but it is argued that the threat of Arab military aggression is acute enough to require that military considerations have priority over all others.

The most effective answer to this policy is to point out that the assumptions on which it is based are not shared either by the British Prime Minister or by the American President. In recent months, American as well as British policy has been based on a quite different assumption—that the nuclear deadlock has made a policy of coexistence between Russia and America inevitable. Are Israeli statesmen prepared to denounce Mr. Macmillan and Mr. Eisenhower as mere "appeasers"? If they are not, they will be driven to the conclusion that the risk of military aggression by the Arabs may not constitute the gravest peril that faces Israel today. In that case it would be worth their taking certain military risks for the sake of relaxing tension in the Middle East, relieving Israel of some of her arms burden and so enabling her to increase the assistance she is already undertaking in the uncommitted areas of the world. Implicit in the policy of East-West coexistence is an ultimate return by Israel to the policy of non-identification.

XIII

At this point, however, it may be useful to dispose of one illusion about non-identification which I shared with many Israelis in the first months after the creation of the state. In those days I was captivated by the concept of Israel as a Middle Eastern Switzerland, dedicated, as the home of three great religions, to a doctrine of eternal neutrality. Whatever the merits of this policy for Swiss democracy, it has been shown during the last decade to be unsuited to the Israeli temper. They have too much red blood in their veins to be capable of the moral self-sufficiency which is required of the professional neutral. Neutrality on the Swiss or Swedish model must be based on an inward-looking national egotism and a calculation of the balance of power which are foreign to the Jewish character. It is no good saying to the Israelis, "Be Swiss," or "Be Swedish," because already, after only ten years, they have developed their own extremely unneutral national character.

But if Israel could never become neutral by free choice and by profession, could it be neutralised by a treaty imposed by the great powers as part of a Middle Eastern system of coexistence? This, after all, is the destiny which the Austrians have accepted, and it is interesting to note that whereas Sweden and Switzerland slowly developed their policies of neutrality, Austria was suddenly neutralised by orders from above. The Austrians are a vital, lively, spontaneous people who (during the Hungarian revolution in 1956, for example) often act in a most unneutral way and feel entitled to do so because they were neutralised, and are not neutral by free choice. This kind of compulsory neutrality might well suit the Israelis too. Suppose that by some miracle the Russians and Americans sat down together and offered a guarantee of the existing frontiers, on condition that Israel never joined a military alliance. I am pretty sure that few responsible Israeli politicians would hesitate to accept the guarantee. It is because this prospect is becoming a little less improbable that it seems to me so important for Israel in the meanwhile to do nothing which would prevent its ultimately coming to fruition.

XIV

The policy of non-identification would, of course, leave Israel free to buy her arms where she will, to have whatever friendships she wishes and to remain ideologically a member of the Western democratic world. Non-identification would merely take care that Israel should not be too closely or too tactlessly associated with either the "Communist" or the "Western imperialist" powers. I deliberately use the clichés accepted in the uncommitted world. Whether they are false is irrelevant, since it is in these terms that Israel's policies will be judged.

It is my personal hope that the Israelis will renew their faith in non-identification—and for two reasons. Firstly, I believe this policy is the framework within which Israel can best fulfill her obligations to the Jews of the Dispersion, including those of the Eastern bloc. In the future as much as in the past, though the funds for immigration will come from the West, the mass of immigrants will come from the East and from the Orient, and no one who has studied recent events in Rumania can exclude the possibility that the Soviet Union could one day permit some at least of its Jewish population to migrate to an Israel which has not been completely integrated into the Western alliance. This is why the attitude of the Israeli democracy in world affairs must always differ from that of the rest of the Western democracies. Israel can never become a mere NATO power or an ordinary member of the Common Market, for the simple reason that the Israelis are not Jews who have ceased to be Jews, but Jews who have returned to Zion while retaining all their Jewish responsibilities.

My second reason for hoping to see a full return to the policy of non-identification is concerned with Israel's new contacts in Asia and Africa. It is one of the most encouraging aspects of the last five years that Israeli statesmen have ceased worrying themselves about the failure to establish any relations with their Arab neighbours and have decided to jump the gap and establish friendship with other inhabitants of underdeveloped areas, such as the Burmese and the people of Ghana. At first it looked as though the advantage gained by the open break with Britain and the war of independence had been entirely dissipated by the Arab boycott and blockade. The good will the Israelis had won among the Asian and African members of the United Nations by their successful liberation from British imperialism disappeared under the stream of Arab and Russian propaganda. Even Pandit Nehru was scared by this agitation into denying Israel full diplomatic recognition and failing to prevent her exclusion from the Bandung Conference.

But recently patient diplomacy has broken through the curtain of isolation with which the Arab blockade has surrounded Israel. It is an admirable example of Asian-Israeli co-operation that seventy Burmese should have arrived in order to learn to run a strategic *kibbutz* on the Chinese frontier. It is equally encouraging to note the number of delegations from Ghana and from French West African dependencies which are visiting Israel in order to learn from her agricultural and social experiments. One should not exaggerate what are only at present modest beginnings, but today it is at least possible to believe that Weizmann's policy of making Israel the pilot plant of the Middle East may now find fulfillment on a far bigger stage. For in providing technical advice to the underdeveloped territories the Israelis have certain advantages over the Western powers. They have no imperial history behind them to create suspicion. On the contrary, they can point to their achievement in throwing off the bonds of imperialism. Furthermore, whereas Britain or France or even America may be suspect in Asia or Africa of using technical aid in order to assist powerful industrial interests, the Israelis can give advice without causing such alarm. Last, but by no means least, I gather that Israeli technical experts are a good deal cheaper to maintain than those from Western countries with higher living standards.

Since the importance of these new contacts with Asia and Africa is undeniable, it surely follows that Israeli foreign policy should be designed to enlarge and strengthen them as fast as possible. Nothing could militate more certainly against achieving this object than the sight of Israel seeking to integrate herself into the Western alliance and working for a military alliance with France, which would identify her lot with that of the white settler.

Of course, if the present relaxation of tension were reversed by a gross act of Communist aggression, Israel too would be compelled to give military strength top priority and obtain what military assistance she could get from the Western powers without regard to the political disadvantages involved. But as long as there is no sign of such developments one must surely hope for a gradual return by Israel to the policy which seemed to express so perfectly Israel's unique position and character when the state was first proclaimed in 1948.

XV

That is really my conclusion. But I wish to add an epilogue. Each day when I was gathering the material for this book, I walked across the beautiful garden from the Weizmann Institute to the Weizmann Archives and sought to persuade Mr. Boris Guriel, the charming chief archivist, to release at least one item from the fantastic treasures he has hoarded in his files. I have reserved to the last perhaps the choicest discovery I made. It is a letter in which Mr. Meyer Weisgal told a friend, in December, 1951, of the last conversation he ever had with Chaim Weizmann and revealed the last message that Weizmann, a few days before his death, gave to the Jewish people. Here, translated from the original Yiddish, are Weizmann's words, which he just managed to whisper to his friend.

"The Jews are a small people, but also a great people. They are an ugly people, but also a beautiful people. They are a people that builds and a people that destroys. They are a people of genius and at the same time a people of enormous stupidity. By their obstinacy they will drive through a wall, but the break in the wall always remains gaping at them."

Then the old man changed the subject and began to talk about science and his beloved Institute. "Those who strive consciously to reach the mountaintop," he whispered, "remain chained to the bottom of the hill. Those who set out to achieve something specific in science never achieve it. It is those who work for science for its own sake who reach the top of the mountain." And then he said these final words: "You have been a loyal friend all the years I have known you. I have other loyal friends, more than I deserve. Tell them not to permit the destruction of the thing we have laboured to build. We Jews can do something very good, something which can be an honour to us all and to all mankind. But we mustn't spoil it. We are an impetuous people and we spoil and sometimes destroy what has taken generations to build up." *

That is what Weizmann said as he died eight years

* For text in Yiddish see Appendix C.

148

ago. I believe that if he could look at what has grown and what has been built since his death, he would still be anxious, but he would also be proud and he would say, "They haven't spoilt it. This is the Jewish state I dreamt of when I was eleven and wrote that letter to my schoolteacher in Motol."

Appendixes

APPENDIX A

Letter written, but never sent, by Weizmann to Churchill

July, 1921

DEAR MR. CHURCHILL,

Before I leave for America, I think that I ought to tell you that there is much uneasiness among Zionists, and to explain, as far as I can, the reasons for it. If I were responsible to English Jews only, my task would be much easier than it is, but as you know, my constituency extends from Singapore to San Francisco and, as you may surmise, in so large an area, there are many cross-currents and a certain amount of suspicion of me because I am a British subject and have identified myself with what may be called the British fulfillment of Zionist hopes. I have never regretted my trust in the word of Great Britain, but for all that my two-fold position as leader of a world-wide movement and as a British subject harnessing the hopes of Zionism to his own country is one of some delicacy. Even if there were no ground of complaint against British policy in Palestine, a merely indulgent interpretation of it would hardly be consistent with my position of trust, and as it is, there are very serious grounds of complaint, as I hope to convince you. You would wish

153

me to speak quite plainly, the more so because I am so often attacked abroad for what is regarded as my undue complaisance to the British policy.

As head of the Zionist movement, I have to think first and last of the success of the cause, but I should not be writing to you now if I did not believe that there was a natural alliance, almost an identity of interest, between Zionism and England in Palestine. Many British statesmen have also taken that view, notably the Prime Minister, Mr. Balfour, and, in certain aspects of policy, yourself; and to these names must be added those of Dominion statesmen such as General Smuts and Sir James Meighen. I have therefore excellent backing for the view that I have taken since the middle and critical periods of the war. On the other hand, there are some amongst us who are beginning to reproach me for what I think you will count as a virtue in a British subject. They say: "The alliance with Great Britain on which you lean is piercing your hand. Great Britain used Zionism to confirm the position won in Palestine by its arms; but, that moral position won, it now scorns the degrees by which it ascended to it, and is about to throw you and your ladder down." This sort of reproach touches in a very sore place, for I have regretfully to admit that recent British policy in Palestine has been disappointing. I want to rebut it, and I submit that if you would enable me to rebut it more decisively than I am able to do at present, you would be doing the British as well as the Zionist cause a great service.

You are, of course, the judge of what is service to England, but when I speak of Jewish Nationalism as a powerful world-force, I speak of what I know. In his last book, *War and Politics,* Ludendorff writes:—

154

The Supreme Command of the Jewish people worked hand in hand with France and England. Maybe it directed both sides. It regarded the coming war as a means of realising its political and economic aims, namely, to obtain for the Jews a state in Palestine, recognition of the Jewish people as a nation, and to secure for it a supreme super-state and super-capitalist position in Europe and America. In order to bring this about, the Jews tried also to obtain the same position in Germany as in those countries which are already in their hands. For this purpose, the Jewish people had to have Germany's defeat.

Zionists do not accept compliments so extravagant and so mixed up with sheer nonsense, but the passage shows that we are regarded as a power. My reading of the war is that it was not altogether in France but in the extreme west and in the east. We helped I think somewhat to the entry of America into the war and to the due recognition of the east as the key to victory. I think it is right to say that our power is on the increase. We represent a political force in America, comparable to the Irish and the Germans, and the hopes of the new constitutional Russia also will depend a great deal on the Jews.

The best beginning of my complaint against present policy in Palestine is in the speech of Sir Herbert Samuel on June 3rd of this year. What the Balfour promise meant, Sir Herbert said, was that some among the Jews, "within the limits that are fixed by the numbers and interests of the present population, should come to Palestine in order to help by their resources and efforts to develop the country to the advantage of all its inhabitants." I can attach no meaning to these words but this, that the

Jewish National Home of the war-promise has now in peace-time been transformed into an Arab national home with such a mixture of prejudices, I say, for there is coupled with this interpretation of the promise, a proposal to establish representative institutions in Palestine which would mean, in present conditions, a great preponderance of Arab members, although the National Home for Jews is supposed to be excluded from their competence, but not the right of the Arab representatives to judge what is in their interests. And it is these interests —not of the future but of the present population—that Sir Herbert Samuel set up as the criterion of the amount of Jewish immigration that may be permitted. Either this proposal to establish representative Government is deceiving the Arabs by offering them something that is nothing at all; or else it mocks us by locking up the promise in a box for safekeeping and giving the key to those whose policy is to keep it there and prevent its ever coming out.

And, as though this injury were not enough in itself, its hurt is increased by the occasion on which it is inflicted. I do not want to exaggerate the stories of Arab outrages on Jews, but I have always desired that as little as possible should be said about them. After all, things just as bad occur in Egypt and India, and nothing is said. What is peculiar to Palestine is that these outrages should actually be used as propaganda against the victims and that Jews in Palestine should be beaten, as it were, with their own crutches. I cannot understand it except in the theory of an anti-Zionist kink in some official minds. Jews who came to Palestine on the strength of a British promise and a Mandate, are made the objects of brutal attacks by the Arabs, and the Government intends to propitiate the Arabs, prohibits the immigration of Jews for a season, and whittles down the Balfour promise to nothing. There is a tremendous gulf. The one speech contemplates immigration on a scale to give the Jews a majority as soon as possible and limited only by the capacity of the country to absorb them; the other speech makes the interests of the present population the criterion of progress; the one constitutes a Palestinian trust for the Jewish people, the other fortifies the Arabs against that trust; the one contemplates a Jewish State, the other a state of Palestine in which there may be Jews. I have been blamed for saying that what we want is a state in Palestine that is Jewish, as England is English. I will so far amend that as to say that we want a Palestine that is Jewish in the sense that Great Britain is English, but that is the irreducible bedrock of our demands. It is not perhaps so much the fault of the High Commissioner having made his speech on June 3rd. The trouble lies deeper (if I may say so). The conditions for his becoming an effectual managing trustee of the British and Zionist interests have not been created. He was given the trust estate with encumbrances which tied the hands of Sir Herbert Samuel or of anyone not endowed with more than ordinary strength and resolution.

Let me explain in more detail what these encumbrances were. The first was a very imperfect sympathy between the military administration and the Zionists. It was natural that the army, or those members which interested themselves in politics, should interest themselves more in the Arabs than in the Jews. The Arabs (not the Arabs of Palestine) had fought on our right flank as a national army; the Jews too had had their military units under General Allenby, but as a race they had been divided by their several national allegiances and for them the late war had the consummate terror of being also a civil war. That the Zionist Organisation had been a protagonist of the Entente, though it is recognised by Ludendorff, was either not known to the political intelligence of the Palestine army or, if known, was held not to count against the undertakings made to Arabs who were regarded as comrades-in-arms and representatives, not of a race, but of a nation. The Government might have enlightened the politicals in the army as to the facts, and it might in making its arrangements with Feisal have stipulated as the condition of his Empire that he should recognise and assist the Zionist policy of the British Government and of the Mandate. Instead, the trouble was exaggerated by making Palestine depend in its military organisation on headquarters in Egypt which are definitely anti-Zionist.

The same insubordination (if I may so call it) was reproduced in the civil administration. You yourself have said that nine-tenths of the officials in Palestine are completely out of sympathy with Zionism. Whose fault was that? I am ready to take my share of the blame, and it is no part of my case to say that we have not made mistakes. No loyal Zionist will be above learning by mistakes, or even receiving correction where his tactics have been faulty. But the main fault was with the Government for not making its policy so plain that it should be impossible for any official to oppose it and still keep his position. The Government thought that they had done their whole duty by appointing Sir Herbert Samuel. But even if he had been stronger than he is, he would still have been powerless to discharge his duty with nine-tenths of his officials opposed to Zionism. We are reproached for not establishing better relations with the Arabs of Palestine. How was that possible with the balance between us oscillating and with the Government on the Hill speaking one policy and the Government in the Plain acting another? This oscillation was an invitation to the Arabs to be restive in the hope that they might further disturb the balance in their own favour. They were not discouraged in Palestine; they have even been encouraged by prominent men in England and in Palestine in their policy of opposition and obstruction. A hero at Government House might perhaps have established equilibrium. But I cannot bring myself to censure Sir Herbert Samuel for not being a superman and carrying off the gates of Gaza on his own back. I realise only too acutely how manifold and world-wide the distractions of the Government have been. Since the peace, devolution of a sort may well have seemed the only way out; but this devolution was on a foundation of sand.

Sir Herbert Samuel's encumbrances became greater, for presently he found himself hampered too by the anti-waste agitation and by the traditional doubts of Liberalism over anything that might by any stretch of the imagination seem to savour of Imperial adventure. I need not enlarge on the theme that the making of new nations is not only work that should be especially congenial to the Liberal spirit but has been a source of strength to this country without which it could not have won the late war. Nor need I dwell on the proposition that this alliance with Zionism is a waxing asset or on the fact well known that the three greatest soldiers of history, Julius Caesar, Alexander and Napoleon, all recognised the immense importance of Palestine in their Eastern schemes and were markedly pro-Jewish in their foreign policy. Napoleon may even be claimed as the first of the modern non-Jewish Zionists. But on the accusation of waste, may I be allowed to offer some considerations? It is a charge that I feel very keenly because the vulgar idea of Jews is that they are all millionaires and the suggestion that they are battening on the poor British taxpayer is very damaging. Believe me, the chief support to Zionism comes not from the rich but from the poor Jews, who, in many cases, by stinting their bodily wants, sustain their ages-old ideal. How can I but be sensitive on their behalf to charges of this nature, resentful of so unjust a slight on their self-denial and jealous in my trusteeship of funds which past sorrows, present sacrifices and faith in England have placed in our hands?

The answer to the charge of waste is threefold. The stock objection to the acquisition of new responsibilities is the speculative character of the economic development, the doubt whether there are the makings in the new country of a state that can stand by itself, and the fear of military commitments. In all these regards the situation in Palestine is exceptionally favourable. You are assured of the influx of a people in which patriotism is already formed and who would feel themselves under a deep obligation to you. You are working with an organisation which is prepared to take a great deal of the financial responsibility for the upbuilding of the country, and finally, if it is the cost of the garrison that appears too high, you could solve it, supposing that all else failed and you cared for that solution, by arming and organising the Jewish colonists. Was a colonisation ever conducted under such favourable conditions that a Government found at its elbow an organisation with a considerable income ready to take over some of its most costly liabilities? In the last year almost a million has been spent in Palestine by Zionists and this money mostly from our people—it represents a great amount of enthusiasm and gratitude.

Secondly, if there were no Palestine, it would, I believe, be necessary to create one in the Imperial interest. It is a bastion to Egypt. On the one side, the existence of a Jewish Palestine leaves you absolutely free to follow whatever policy may be most convenient to you, and enables you, if you wished, to evacuate Egypt altogether and to concentrate in the Canal Zone with your army based on Palestine. The real defence of Egypt against foreign enemies is at sea and on land in Palestine, and if one was paying three times as much on the military garrison of Palestine one would be purchasing these strategic advantages very cheaply.

Lastly, you have set up a great Arab kingdom in Mesopotamia, but for all that, you will have to rely in Palestine on the Jews for your loyal element. It is an asset on which you can draw almost indefinitely in case of danger. Why quote figures of the present population when behind the minority of Jews in Palestine stand the hundreds of thousands of patriotic Jews ready to die for you if you will be the founder and faithful protector of Zion? In building upon that you build upon a rock. Almost alone amongst political organisations, the Zionist movement has emerged from the war more united than ever and with increased strength and resources. It is difficult to understand how one can build on Arab loyalty so near the vital communications across the Isthmus of Suez. All one has seen and heard of the Arab movement leads one to believe that it is anti-European.

The Palestine-Zionist policy, far from being waste, becomes a necessary insurance that we quote to you at a lower rate than anyone else could dream of.

Please do not think that I am unmindful of the difficulties in Palestine or that I want to press the logic of an argument beyond the limits of what is reasonable and practicable. If I were assured that the substance of what we want was ours, I would gladly make any or every surrender of form that might be dictated by prudence and, as you know, I am willing to consent to make arrangements with Arabs that would guarantee them every security for their civil and religious rights. But what I fear is that the forms are ours, the substance theirs, and I write to beg of you not to throw away the substance for the shadow of strength, not to buy temporary accommodation at the cost of permanent accession of strength and it might be (if the promise were not kept) at the price of honour, and, finally, to take a lesson from the Turks, who maintained order in Palestine with three men and a boy. Why? Because they knew their own minds, miserable as they were, and never suffered an ambiguity to infect their policy. You can do the same if you know your own minds and act on the awe that your settled will inspires everywhere in the world.

Permit me to state precisely what in our opinion is wanted. I want—or rather we want—for I speak for the greatest of single constituencies—

(1) the Mandate,
(2) the purging of the Palestine Civil Service of every insubordinate who will not work for the Mandate,
(3) a public exposition of the value of Palestine to the British position in the east,
(4) a declaration by Feisal in favour of the Mandate,

(5) a recognition of the principle of equal representation of Jews and Arabs in Palestine in any representative system that may be set up and a clear understanding that the interest of Jewry in the country is world-wide and not defined by the numbers of the present Jewish colonists; and

(6) a Concordat with the Arabs which I think I can obtain if the previous conditions are satisfied, but not if they are not.

APPENDIX B

Letter from Weizmann to the Chief Rabbi of Palestine

21st July, 1946

MY DEAR CHIEF RABBI,

I was deeply interested in the detailed report you were good enough to give me this morning of your conversations with the Archbishop of Canterbury and Mr. Attlee, and am most grateful to you for all the trouble you have taken. You mentioned that you hoped to see His Grace again, and asked me whether I could give you a brief outline of my views on the present situation in Palestine, and on the action which I believe should be taken in order to remedy it.

I am complying with your request in haste, and without consultation, so that what follows represents my own personal views. Moreover, I have only just arrived in this country, and am not yet recovered from the shock of the last few weeks in Palestine, or from a hurried journey, so I hope you will forgive any gaps or other signs of haste in what follows.

(1) Palestine today is not merely a police state: it is the worst form of military dictatorship. To all intents and purposes there is no Civil Administration; that has receded entirely into the background, and my impression is that the country is run by military cliques in Jerusalem

165

and/or Cairo. This has been the case for some time now, but has recently, of course, become more obvious, and the present situation is hopeless. Anybody may be arrested by any soldier or officer, without warrant, without reason given; he can be thrown into custody, and kept there till the military choose to bring a charge, institute a trial or enquiry—or at their pleasure release him. He has no redress. In Palestine today the writ of habeas corpus does not run. There is a severe censorship—both on press messages abroad and on the local papers, and no freedom of comment in the press. The prisons and camps are thronged with people arrested on the flimsiest pretexts, some of whom have already languished there for months, and none of whom has any certainty as to when he will be brought to trial or released.

I am informed that the G.O.C. [General Officer Commanding] Palestine is credited with having said that he would like to "uproot every Jew in Palestine." This story was, I believe, telegraphed here by the distinguished British journalist who mentioned it to me (he was in Palestine recently), but received no publicity. I believe it to be true; certainly it is supported by the type of "propaganda" known to be current among British troops in Palestine, who are being taught to regard the Jews as "the enemy." When search was made on June 29th at Givat Brenner (a village only a few minutes by car from Rehovoth, so I can vouch for what happened there), the troops had been told they were to "occupy" it, and they behaved accordingly. They began to break into the schoolrooms and into a small laboratory which the children use; they broke into the girls' dormitory; pilfered watches, fountain-pens and other trinkets; tore or cut up clothing stored for the use of the *chalutzim,* and generally behaved like "conquerors." Characteristic of the whole proceedings here were the slogans used by the "invaders": "What we need is gas-chambers!" "Hitler didn't finish the job!" Swastikas were chalked or painted on walls (and also even on the pavements of Rehovoth—where I have seen them with my own eyes!). Everything was characteristic of troops preparing for "The Day."

(2) It has been stated by the authorities that there was no intention in these searches of damaging the country's economy. It is difficult to believe this in view of the fact that in many settlements the whole male population has been carried away into detention, and is being kept in custody throughout the period of the harvest. It is my own view that, contrary to the official statements, the deliberate intention in these operations was to destroy as many of the settlements as possible. I believe that the recent operations were intended as the preliminary stage of something much larger. The military cliques expected a violent reaction to their first effort, a reaction such as would have justified the use of artillery, the bombing of Tel Aviv and other centres, and so on. But this was realised by the Yishuv, and although they were and are burning with indignation at the iniquities and indignities inflicted on them, they decided not to be "drawn," and maintained great restraint and rigorous discipline throughout. I think that perhaps Mr. Sacher and myself, who have seen almost all the leading representatives of the Yishuv, may have had something to do with this state of affairs, which I hope may endure for a little while yet. But no one should be under any illusions: a state of tension such as exists today among the Jews of Palestine cannot last long. I have warned the High Commissioner about this, in no uncertain terms. What is likely to hap-

pen, if no hope is held out, if the leaders are not soon released, is that the Haganah will split, and the younger elements will join the more extreme terrorist groups. And then, may God help us all! Before my departure I had already heard people say: "Rather die fighting than turn Vichy."

(3) So the urgency today is very great. The British will soon find themselves in the position of having to shoot down thousands of Jews in Palestine. I don't think such action will help them much; nor do I relish the prospect from our own point of view. That is why I urge once again:

(A) the release of the members of the Agency Executive now under detention;

(B) the grant of the 100,000 certificates; and

(c) the re-establishment of the Civil Authority in Palestine.

As regards the last point, the military clique is a danger not only to the Jews of Palestine, but also to British interests throughout the Middle East. There is some resemblance between the situation in Palestine today and that in France at the time of the Dreyfus affair—except that in Palestine it is on a larger scale, and on much more dangerous ground. Yet the Republic of France was shaken to its foundations by the *affaire Dreyfus;* I fear the position of the British in the Middle East may come into very grave danger through the position in Palestine now.

(4) I have been able to give above only a very brief sketch of what seem to me the salient factors in a complex situation, and indicated what I think must be done as a short-term policy to relieve present tension. But that is not all, and I would like to add a word or two about

the possible long-term solution.

(5) When the Report of the Anglo-American Committee appeared, I was in favour of its acceptance, and so were most of my colleagues of the Executive of the Jewish Agency, though we all realised that the Report had its lacunae, and even its negative side. But we did see in it the possibility of resuming constructive work, and my own belief in the value of constructive effort is so great that I was convinced that it would heal all wounds in time, and that time, too, would iron out most of the defects in the programme. Because I have myself more faith in Divine Prophecy than in the opinions of any twelve good men and true—however well-intentioned —I advised my friends very strongly to accept the Report as it stood, start work on that basis, and wait for better days.

But I am afraid that since the events of Saturday, June 29th, the situation has changed fundamentally. Something has definitely snapped in the relationship between Jews and British in Palestine, and I, as a firm believer in, and champion of, that relationship, am forced to realise that what has been destroyed is so deep, so vital and of such moral significance, that it cannot be restored by projects, resolutions, and kind words.

I feel, therefore, that the only thing is to revert now to the Peel Report, which admitted that the British could not rule over the Jews, and that the only way to establish normal relations between the two peoples is to partition Palestine, and set up an independent Jewish State in treaty relations with Great Britain. What was true in 1937 is true, *a fortiori,* today, and it is the only way in which the situation may yet be saved. I am not unmindful of the difficulties—but they are trivial compared with the difficulties of keeping the Yishuv under British Administration. After partition, there may be a chance of good relations developing again. Nothing else can clear the air now. What has happened in Palestine has been burnt into the soul of every man, woman and child in the Yishuv.

(6) I do not wish to make this statement any longer than I must, but I should like to add a word about the Arab question. In spite of all the advice of the experts (who have mostly proved to be sworn enemies of the Jews), and in spite of the vituperations of certain Arab princes, I am convinced that once a Jewish State has been established the Arabs and the Jews will have to get together on the basis of their common interests. I do not wish at the moment to give chapter and verse for my conviction on this subject, for I would not wish to compromise any of my Arab friends, but I am not speaking without good reason. The so-called "experts" on Arab affairs are frightened to put the thing to the test. The same fear dominates Mr. Bevin and the Foreign Office—coupled with the anti-Semitism which shows through their utterances on Zionism and Zionist affairs.

I must apologise for the length of this letter, as well as for any carelessness in the phrasing; as I explained, I write in haste, and am not revising. You will, I know, bear this in mind in any use you may make of it.

APPENDIX C

Weizmann's last conversation with Weisgal

Yidden sainen a klein Folk, ober a groiss Folk. Sei sainen a miess Folk, ober oich a Schein Folk. Sei sainen a Folk wos boit un a Folk wos zerstert. Sei sainen a genialer Folk, un zu selber Zeit a narrisch Folk. In seier Akshoness-digkeit sei kennen durch brechen a Wand, ober der Lock in Wand wet stendig blaiben kukendig oif sei. . . .

Die, welche streben bawustsinnig zu dergraichen dem Gipfel fun Barg, wellen farblaiben wie zugekeit zum Yissod fun Barg. Jene, welche farsuchen zu dergraichen wos-nit-is speziell in Wissenschaft, konnen keinmol gornischt derzielen. Nor jene, welche horrewen far di Wissenschaft l'Schmoi, wellen dergraichen dem oiberschten fun Barg. . . .

Ihr seint gewesen mein traier Fraind sint ich kenn Aich. Ich hob oich andere traie Fraind, mer Fraind wi ich fardien. Sogt sei, l'ma'an Haschem, sei sollen nischt derlosen choirew zu machen die Sach, welche Doiress hoben gehorrewet oifzuboien. Mir Yidden sainen messugel zu schaffen a sehr scheine Sach, a Sach, welche kenn sein a Kowed far uns allemen un far die ganze Menschheit. Ober mir torren nit kalle machen. Mir seinen an "Ame Psise" un amol machen mir kalle un take zersteren an Oiftu, wos hot genummen Doiress oifzuboien.

171

RICHARD H. S. CROSSMAN

lives in London, where he was born on December 15, 1907. He attended Winchester College and New College, Oxford, where he was a fellow and tutor of politics from 1930 to 1937. A Labour Party Member of Parliament, Mr. Crossman began his political career in 1934 as Leader of the Labour Group on Oxford City Council, serving for six years. From 1938 to 1940 he was a Lecturer for Oxford University Delegacy for Extra Mural Studies and Workers' Educational Association. He served as Deputy Director of Psychological Warfare, AFHQ, Algiers, in 1943, and from 1944 to 1945 as Assistant Chief of Psychological Warfare Division of SHAEF. The following year he served on the Anglo-American Palestine Commission, and in 1955 participated in the Malta Round Table Conference. Assistant editor of *New Statesman and Nation* from 1938 to 1955, Mr. Crossman has written articles for *New Statesman* and *Encounter*. His books include PLATO TODAY, GOVERNMENT AND THE GOVERNED, PALESTINE MISSION, and THE CHARM OF POLITICS.

The subtitle of Mr. Crossman's book neatly expresses both its content and quality. He was, in his own words, "pitched into the Palestine problem," first as an observer, when in 1945 he became one of the two British MP's on the Anglo-American Commission of Enquiry, and later as a participant, when in the three tempestuous years that culminated in the declaration of Israeli independence he headed the active opposition in the British Parliament to Ernest Bevin's disastrous policy.

Reflecting on those years, he now feels this birth of a nation to be the greatest democratic achievement since World War II and, incidentally, the most thrilling episode in his own lively political life. This personal account, indeed, is